BREAK A SWEAT, CHANGE YOUR LIFE

The Urgent Need for Physical Education in Schools

WILLIAM E. SIMON JR.

authorHOUSE®

AuthorHouse™
1663 Liberty Drive
Bloomington, IN 47403
www.authorhouse.com
Phone: 1 (800) 839-8640

Published by AuthorHouse 07/02/2018

ISBN: 978-1-5462-4367-0 (sc)
ISBN: 978-1-5462-4366-3 (hc)
ISBN: 978-1-5462-4365-6 (e)

Library of Congress Control Number: 2018906628

Print information available on the last page.

This book is printed on acid-free paper.

Advance Praise for
Break a Sweat, Change Your Life

[T]he current levels of obesity and inactivity in our children have become the most fearful enemies to their health. ... *Break a Sweat, Change Your Life* thoughtfully and constructively addresses the health crisis today's children are facing, calling on schools to implement adequate physical education programs at all grade levels in order to give our youth a strong start in life.

> From the foreword by Kenneth H. Cooper, MD, MPH, "the Father of Aerobics"

Break a Sweat, Change Your Life takes a much-needed look at the deplorable lack of physical education in our nation's schools, identifying the science behind the need for robust PE programs, as well as ways to improve the situation. Bill Simon has spent decades attempting to revitalize physical education in schools, and everyone who cares about children should read his book.

> John J. Ratey, MD,
> Associate Clinical Professor of Psychiatry at Harvard Medical School and author of *Spark: The Revolutionary New Science of Exercise and the Brain*

One of the best things we can do for our children is to make exercise a routine part of their lives. This is a highly readable, informative book that explains the huge physical, cognitive, and mental health benefits our children gain when we help them to stay active.

> Wendy A. Suzuki, PhD,
> Professor of Neural Science and Psychology at New York University and author of *Healthy Brain, Happy Life*

A significant amount of scientific research has demonstrated that brains, minds, and bodies of the young all benefit from exercise. Outstanding physical education programs will give middle school and high school students the skills, knowledge, and motivation to stay fit over their lifetimes. Bill Simon makes an excellent case that physical education should be valued as highly as academic studies in our schools.

Ming Guo, MD, PhD,

Professor in Neurology and Pharmacology at UCLA David Geffen School of Medicine

Physical education means more than exercise. It means providing children with the knowledge and understanding they need to lead healthy lives through adequate exposure to the only subject in school that nurtures the body, mind, and spirit of students. Read this book, and learn what we all need to know to help grow sound minds and sound bodies for the sake of our country's future.

John Naber, 1976 Olympic champion swimmer, broadcaster, author, and speaker

For physical education teachers everywhere, with gratitude for all they do to equip future generations to lead healthy lives

Contents

Foreword

In the period 1976 to 1980, 5.5 percent of American children two to nineteen years of age were obese, with 11 percent being overweight or obese. However, between 2015 and 2016, the numbers dramatically increased, with 18 percent obese and 36 percent overweight or obese. That puts America in a position of having more overweight children than any other country in the world!

Along with this obesity epidemic, there has been a marked increase in type 2 diabetes, which was a rarity forty years ago. I believe the reasons for these statistics are as follows:

- There are not enough physical education programs in schools.
- Children don't walk or ride their bicycles to school as they used to.
- They are spending six to eight hours on daily screen time.
- They are eating extensively at fast-food restaurants.

I believe it is safe to say that the current levels of obesity and inactivity in our children have become the most fearful enemies to their health. Unless we do something in the immediate future, we will be facing a health-care crisis that could bankrupt this country within a few years.

Realizing the critical need for improving the health of our children, in 2007 I tried to pass a state law (SB-530) that for the first time in many years would bring PE back into Texas schools. With the No Child Left Behind program, PE was replaced with math, science, and reading in an effort to improve academic grades. It didn't work, and we now know that the best way to improve academic performance is to improve children's level of fitness (see chapter 3). I testified four times during that legislative session in 2007, trying to get SB-530 passed, but I faced considerable resistance. At first, many parents rebelled because they "didn't want the government any more involved in their private lives than they already were," with which I totally agreed. Nevertheless, I told the parents, "In the area of fitness and obesity, you have failed miserably since in Texas we rank as having some of the fattest and most deconditioned children in the United States!"

Then the politicians were less than supportive. They said, "We don't have the money to bring PE back into the school!" It would take at least three million dollars to equip all nine thousand schools in Texas with the FitnessGram testing equipment, which was also a requirement of SB-530, and train twenty-five thousand teachers how to not only give the test but also to become qualified to be PE teachers.

However, by June 2007, former Governor Rick Perry signed SB-530 into law as a "mandate without funding"! I told the legislature, "If the state won't fund this project, I will raise enough private funds to meet the requirements." With a lot of hard work by dedicated people, we raised $3.1 million by January 2008. PE was brought back into the schools for grades K–12, and FitnessGram testing was required annually for grades three through twelve.

Our results in testing more than 2.4 million children that spring and reporting them in the newspapers "shook up" the state since the results were unbelievably poor. However, since "data drives decision," we have now seen a turnaround in the fitness and obesity problems in our Texas children and "the rest is history."

I tell this story because our project is only ten years old, but Bill Simon's program is celebrating twenty years of combating obesity and inactivity in 141 (and growing) underserved middle and high schools, mostly in the Los Angeles area. Moreover, his challenges in implementing and funding these schools were comparable to what we have experienced in Texas.

Therefore, on this twentieth anniversary of the UCLA Health Sound Body Sound Mind organization, I am both honored and delighted to be asked to contribute to this book and hope it will stimulate more interest in Bill's program. *Break a Sweat, Change Your Life* thoughtfully and constructively addresses the health crisis today's children are facing, calling on schools to implement adequate physical education programs at all grade levels in order to give our youth a strong start in life.

Congratulations, Bill, and I hope that you will enjoy even greater success in the next twenty years. Through our combined efforts, we can look forward to a healthier America.

Kenneth H. Cooper, MD, MPH

Introduction: Giving Kids the Chance They Deserve

Everyone knows that physical fitness is a good thing, so if you are holding this book in your hand, you may be wondering what you could possibly learn from it. In fact, there is lots of news about the myriad benefits of physical activity and, conversely, the significant dangers of inactivity. Gone are the days when getting daily exercise was considered optional, something to aspire to, perhaps, but about as important as eating your spinach. Today we know that ignoring your body's need for exercise not only puts you at risk for major disease that will shorten your life but also deprives you of doing and feeling your best mentally and emotionally.

This is true for children as well as adults—especially children whose potential for long life can be enhanced or diminished by the choices they make and we make for them. Youth offers only short-term protection from the diseases that accompany obesity* and inactivity, which often have their roots in childhood. In addition, today's high-pressure childhoods cry out for every cognitive and emotional advantage that fitness can provide. Unfortunately, a perfect storm of circumstances has conspired to minimize physical activity in our children's lives, thus depriving them of the benefits we now know exercise confers and

---

* Obesity is a term we will use often in this book. In simplest terms, obesity is defined as abnormal or excessive fat accumulation that may impair health. More technically, if an individual's body mass index (BMI) is over thirty, he or she is obese. To calculate BMI, divide a person's weight (in pounds) by height (in inches) squared, and then multiply that number by a conversion factor of 703.

propelling them deeper into the abyss of inactivity with its attendant risks. If we had deliberately tried to set up the next generation for a health crisis, I doubt we could have been more effective.

How is it that in our child-centric country, where schools and parents work mightily to remove every perceived risk from children's lives, we are stripping them of what is arguably their best chance at good health?

It doesn't have to be this way. While some of the root causes of our children's physical inactivity are difficult to address, none of them is beyond us to correct. My special focus, the area in which I am most experienced and where I believe we can have the most impact, is our schools. This is where almost all children spend most of their waking hours and where decisions adults make can be most consequential.

Accordingly, I believe significant responsibility rests with schools to provide children with a good start in life and to equip them with the knowledge they need to live healthy lives. This requires, more than ever, effective physical education classes. Unfortunately, PE has slipped to the bottom of the curricular ladder in all too many schools. While I appreciate the competing concerns schools must prioritize, it is time to move physical education to an upper rung as a core subject, as important as any academic endeavor such as math, history, or English.

Americans everywhere agree that children have a right to a quality education, as a number of state constitutions and courts have recognized. I believe physical education is a fundamental aspect of that right. To succeed in the world, a child must know how to stay healthy. Moreover, a child cannot develop to his or her full potential without engaging in the kind of physical activities that teach character, team work, self-respect, and fair play.

If we don't give physical education a more central place in the curriculum, we are jeopardizing our children's future as surely as if we were buying them daily packs of cigarettes.

While the immediate impetus for this book is my concern for the health of America's children and for our country's future, it also stems from the way physical fitness has made such a huge difference in my own life. I would like to share a little of my background in the hope that this will help others appreciate the benefits of fitness.

Although I played organized sports all through high school and college, I was hardly a star athlete and had little interest in fitness for its own sake. You weren't going to find me at the gym lifting weights or doing crunches. However, I was naturally quite competitive and, like most kids, craved the sense of identity and pride that comes with being good at something. I particularly enjoyed racquet sports, including tennis and squash. I played primarily to have fun and because I liked the camaraderie of my teammates. I certainly wasn't thinking about all the physical and mental benefits of exercise. At twenty, I was blessed with good health and was naive enough to take it for granted.

But I did know one thing: when I played an intense game of tennis or squash, I felt great. I felt more energetic, both physically and intellectually, after I finished a match. It was exhilarating, even when we lost. Although I could not have told you why at the time, I also did better academically when I was playing on a team. Today there is significant research on the cognitive benefits of physical exercise, as I'll discuss later, but back then, all I knew was that exercise made me more positive and productive. When I finished a game of tennis or squash, I was ready to tackle my academics with renewed energy and a clear head.

After graduating from college, I worked in Manhattan for several years and did not make as much time for sports or exercise as I used to. It was not until my last year in law school in 1982 that I truly got back in shape. Two classmates and I decided we wanted to run the Boston Marathon, which takes place each year on Patriots' Day, the third Monday in April. This meant we would have to train in January, February, and March, when it was cold, damp, and dark in New England. Of course, it was a terrific incentive to have two buddies to jog with, but I don't think I'd have made it through those months if I didn't feel so great once I got back from a run. The cold really wasn't a factor once I warmed up, and I could ignore the elements because I felt fantastic afterward.

Soon I had discovered a new organizing principle for my life: regular exercise could help me live stronger in every way, physically, cognitively, and emotionally. Over the years, I have found many ways to exercise, from workouts at the gym to hiking and mountain climbing. Regular exercise has been a constant in my life. It's the rare day that I don't get any, and I feel it when I don't—mentally as well as physically.

As I was getting in shape for the Boston Marathon, I learned my first life lesson based on my new fitness regimen: good habits rewire your brain to achieve your goals. Once I committed to the training, I noticed something. After a couple of weeks, it wasn't as hard to get motivated anymore. Sure, there were cold and wet days when I would rather have stayed home, but running had become a habit and I didn't argue with myself when it was time to go out. Good habits put us on automatic pilot to do what we should and are essential components of lives well lived.

Second, exercise made me push myself. In fitness, as is the case with so much of life, you get out of it what you put in, and the determination it took to reach my fitness goals primed me to succeed in other ways. This may seem like an obvious lesson, that if you push yourself you'll be more successful in facing life's challenges, but again, it's all about habit. If you are in the habit of pushing yourself, you're bound to succeed a good bit of the time. And you will look at the world in a different way. You'll see more opportunities and fewer obstacles.

The third life lesson I learned from fitness is related to the second. It's about resilience. If you push yourself physically, it's a sure bet you are going to suffer setbacks. I experienced many (happily, fairly minor) injuries over the years, such as when I hurt my hip training for the New York City Marathon in 2008. In order to compete, I needed to push through some pain and find a gentler way to train. So I began "running" in a swimming pool without touching my feet to the bottom. Experiences like this brought home the realization that with some resolve and resourcefulness, I could cross the finish line in many other areas of life. Keeping fit over a period of years teaches resilience because you know you can meet adversity and move beyond it.

I became a real believer in the transformative power of physical fitness a long time ago. Over the years, as I grew in material success and was able to be more involved in charitable causes, I always looked for opportunities related to fitness and health as well as education.

Overall, I have devoted most of my effort to programs focusing on youth, for I believe a good start in life is a springboard to a bright future. As a squash enthusiast, I joined the urban squash movement as soon as I heard about it, serving as chair for eleven years of the Squash + Education Alliance (formerly known as the National Urban Squash and Education Association). There are now twenty-three urban squash programs in major cities in the United States and abroad, offering inner-city students intensive after-school, weekend, and summer programming that includes not only squash but also mentoring, academic tutoring, community service, college placement, and more.

Squash has often been described as a physical chess game played against four walls, so it is a mentally stimulating sport as well as a physically challenging one. Of urban squash students who stay in our programs, 96 percent graduate from high school and enroll in college,[1] which to me is corroboration of current research showing how exercise improves academic outcomes.

In contrast to the off-campus programs of urban squash, in 1998 my wife, Cindy, and I founded a school-based fitness program in Los Angeles, which we called Sound Body Sound Mind. Over the past twenty years, Sound Body Sound Mind has grown to serve over 160,000 kids a year in 127 of our city's public middle and high schools.

In 2015, we joined forces with UCLA Health, one of the largest and most advanced health-care systems in the world, in order to bring to bear the resources and expertise of both organizations on the issue of adolescent health. Our program is cost-effective, scalable, and based on a straightforward idea: give schools a range of fitness equipment and train PE teachers in a curriculum all students enjoy, and fitness levels will soar—as well academic performance. Our goal at UCLA Health Sound Body Sound Mind stretches far beyond the school years, however. Ultimately, we want to give children the skills, knowledge, confidence, and motivation they need to stay fit over their lifetimes.

In the twenty years since we launched Sound Body Sound Mind, I have learned a lot about physical education in public schools and about children's fitness and health more generally. This has involved some shocking revelations that confirm the magnitude of the problem Dr. Cooper describes in his foreword. Among them are the following:

- About one-third of American children are overweight.[2] Many of these are obese, not just overweight. Between 2015–2016, some one in five children ages six to nineteen were obese, with 14 percent of younger children, ages two to five, falling into this category.[3] Moreover, overweight children stand an 80 percent chance of being overweight as adults.[4]
- Pediatricians are treating a host of diseases in children, such as type 2 diabetes and hypertension, which used to be considered adult problems.[5] The present generation of American children may become the first to live shorter lifespans than their parents.[6]
- The Department of Health and Human Services guidelines recommend one hour of moderate to vigorous physical activity for six to seventeen year olds seven days a week.[7] Yet only 21.6 percent of children and adolescents get sixty minutes of physical activity even five days per week.[8]
- Despite the overwhelming evidence that physical activity reduces the risk of chronic illness and improves academic

outcomes, the median PE budget for American schools is $764.[9] *That's no typo.* Under $800 a year for a whole school.

In light of the grave health risks that obesity and inactivity pose to our children, it is of enormous concern to me that so many school policy makers regard physical education as an "extra" of marginal importance to a school's academic purpose. There is nothing "marginal" or unimportant about physical education and the physical fitness it promotes. It is essential not only for good health but also for many positive spillover effects, some of which I described earlier based on my own experience, which will strengthen children as individuals and prepare them for productive lives and the inevitable challenges they will face.

Readers will note that my book focuses quite a bit on obesity as well as on physical activity. Whether obesity causes inactivity or inactivity promotes obesity is the subject of much debate, but there is a clear correlation between the two. My guess is that the relationship runs both ways. In other words, children who don't get enough activity gain weight, but then once they are heavier, they are less inclined to be active. In any event, it would be almost impossible to write about fitness without reference to the obesity epidemic our nation faces.

As UCLA Health Sound Body Sound Mind celebrates its twentieth anniversary, I feel compelled to speak out more publicly on the dangers of childhood inactivity and to underscore the benefits of an active lifestyle, both academic and otherwise. In order to give our children the healthy start they deserve in life and to prepare them to pursue fitness as adults, it is imperative that our schools offer more physical education. Schools are in a unique position to teach our children how important fitness is.

Happily, many people have long been working toward the same end, so I am simply standing on their shoulders. I am grateful that several of them have contributed to this book.

In the following pages, we'll get a public health overview of the dangers of sedentary lifestyles and unhealthy eating from Dr. Jonathan Fielding, former director of the Los Angeles County Department of Public Health, and we'll hear from Dr. Kenneth Cooper, "the Father of Aerobics," about the deadly duo of obesity and inactivity. Dr. John Ratey, a neuroscientist and author of the best-selling book *Spark: The Revolutionary New Science of Exercise and the Brain*,[10] will discuss what he has learned about the wonder drug that is physical activity. We will consider the state of PE around the country with the help of Dr. Frances Cleland, president of SHAPE America, the Society of Health and Physical Educators. Two award-winning physical education teachers—John Kruse and Christine Berni-Ramos—will share their experience from the classroom with us, and we will also hear from the former director of student medical services for the Los Angeles County Unified School District, Dr. Kimberly Uyeda. Toward the end of the book, we will look at several local and national programs working to improve physical education and will give some suggestions as to how the reader might become involved in this effort.

In addition, I want to tell you about the history of UCLA Health Sound Body Sound Mind, both as a way of celebrating its accomplishments in the past twenty years and as an example of a simple, successful program that could be easily replicated anywhere.

By the time you finish this book, I hope you will have a better appreciation of how crucial physical education is for America's children and will join me in calling for a changed mindset that values it as greatly as any academic subject in our schools. Our country boasts one of the highest standards of living in the world, and we must find a way to give our kids the gift of physical education and fitness. This is one of the most important things we can do to ensure that the next generation enjoys that same standard of living as well as a longer life expectancy.

1

SEDENTARY LIFESTYLES AND UNHEALTHY EATING: THE PUBLIC HEALTH PERSPECTIVE

Today's sedentary lifestyle is a recent phenomenon in human history. Regular vigorous physical activity was a necessity for primitive man, who had to hunt, gather, and eventually farm his food. The ancient civilizations of China, Persia, and India all understood the health benefits of physical activity.[1] Susruta of India, who lived around 600 BC, may have been the first physician to recommend moderate daily exercise to his patients.[2] He proclaimed that "diseases fly from the presence of a person habituated to regular physical exercise."[3] In the East Han dynasty of China, a surgeon named Hua T'O (c. 140-208 AD) prescribed "frolic exercises" for his patients, which mimicked the movements of deer, tigers, bears, cranes, and monkeys.[4]

But perhaps no civilization has esteemed physical fitness so highly as the ancient Greeks. After all, they did invent the Olympic Games, which continue to captivate attention as the world's premier celebration of physical achievement. The Spartans placed a huge emphasis on physical fitness and endurance, requiring rigorous physical training for all males in order to produce highly fit warriors.[5] By contrast, in Athens, Hippocrates (c. 460–375 BC) extolled exercise for its overall healthful benefits, writing that "eating alone will not keep a man well; he must also take exercise."[6] He was the first physician we know of to give a written prescription for exercise to a patient.[7]

Fitness was also a highly valued part of a good education. The Greeks believed a strong body and a sound mind were closely linked, so they emphasized physical training as a fundamental part of every boy's schooling.[8] Plato (c. 428-348 BC), who was a particularly skilled wrestler, advocated sport to build character and, along with music, to bring harmony to the soul.[9] For Plato, athletics cultivated the attributes needed—endurance, focus, and perseverance—to progress toward knowledge and wisdom.[10]

The Romans also placed a premium on physical fitness. Like the Spartans, they valued fitness more for its military application than for any intrinsic appreciation of sport or mind/body balance. During the glory years of the Roman Empire, all Roman citizens between the ages of seventeen and sixty were eligible for the draft, so they needed to be physically ready for military service.[11] Such training included running, marching, jumping, and discus and javelin throwing.[12] But Roman physicians, especially Claudius Galenus, known as Galen (c. 130-200 A.D.), did recognize the usefulness of exercise in medical treatment, and his thinking remained influential until the end of the Middle Ages.[13] As Rome became richer and its people more self-indulgent, eventually the Roman Empire fell in 476 AD. People have debated the reasons for Rome's decline ever since. Many factors undoubtedly led to the demise of its civilization, but one of them was surely its army's declining physical condition. According to Flavius Vegetius Renatus, who wrote a treatise on the Roman system of warfare around 400 AD:

> Footsoldiers [*sic*] wore breastplates and helmets. But when, because of negligence and laziness, parade ground drills were abandoned, the customary armour began to seem heavy, since the soldiers rarely wore it. Therefore, they asked the emperor to set aside first the breastplates and mail, and then the helmets. So our soldiers fought the Goths without any protection for chest and head and were often beaten by archers. Although there were many disasters, which led to the

loss of great cities, no one tried to restore breastplates and helmets to the infantry. Thus it happens that troops in battle, exposed to wounds because they have no armour, think about running and not about fighting.[14]

Fast-forward from ancient Rome to the early years of our own country, when fitness was a functional requirement as we pioneered and settled the land. Felling trees, clearing rocks and underbrush, walking long distances, rowing down rivers, and building homes from what stone and wood could be found all demanded a high level of physical fitness and mental fortitude. Thomas Jefferson wrote extensively about the importance of exercise, recommending people give "about two of them [hours] every day to exercise, for health must not be sacrificed to learning. A strong body makes the mind strong."[15]

We seem to have lost the wisdom of past generations when it comes to physical fitness, and as a result, we are imperiling the nation's future.

A public health visionary speaks out

Happily, there are many key leaders today, Dr. Jonathan Fielding prominent among them, who are striving to recapture the ancients' appreciation for physical fitness. Dr. Fielding clearly revels in his work as one of the country's most distinguished experts on public health. However, even after a long and storied career, he is not content to rest on his laurels. "We still have such an enormous preventable burden of disease. While we have made progress, it's important not to be satisfied and always to look ahead to what more can be accomplished to improve our individual and community health," he says.[16]

As a professor at UCLA, Dr. Fielding, with his public health mentor, Dr. Lester Breslow, developed a data-driven course on the determinants of health in populations. To this effort, he brought sixteen years of experience as the visionary founding director of the Los Angeles County Department of Public Health. No fewer than five academic degrees and several decades of service have shaped Dr. Fielding's perspective on public health. UCLA's School of Public Health was named after Dr. Fielding and his wife in 2012.

As a high school student, Dr. Fielding won a competition that enabled him to be "director of public health for a day" in the populous suburb of Westchester County, just outside of New York City. This experience, although brief, introduced him to a broader view of health than the practice of medicine provides, one concerned with the health of populations and the differences among subpopulations. Still, after completing Harvard Medical School in 1969, he set out to become a pediatrician because he felt that by caring for children, he could have a positive long-term impact on their health as adults.

During his training, he found that many of his patients' problems arose from poverty, food insufficiency, neglect, and violence, which he felt helpless to solve in clinical practice. As a result, he decided he wanted to tackle systemic issues like these rather than care for individual patients. So he returned to Harvard for his master's degree in public health and took up work as medical director for the US Department of Labor's Job Corps. There, he was responsible for the health of fifty thousand adolescents and adults per year living in Job Corps residential centers, hoping to get high school equivalency certification and training for jobs with marketable skills. "These were mostly high school dropouts who came from very difficult, often desperate circumstances," Dr. Fielding told *UCLA Public Health* magazine. "You could see the effects of poverty and other social forces on their life trajectory, and the importance of prevention. It made me think hard about what I wanted to do, and it just seemed logical that if I wanted to really make a difference at a broad level, I should go into the direction of public health."[17]

And make a difference he did. At the Los Angeles County Department of Public Health, his many accomplishments included a reduction in tobacco use, better emergency preparedness, efforts to bring down the threat of lead poisoning in low-income areas, and a restaurant grading system that reduced restaurant-related foodborne illness outbreaks and hospitalizations by up to 20 percent. He and his team also developed programs to increase physical activity among county residents and halt the increase in the childhood obesity rate.[18]

Obesity's life-threatening and preventable consequences

Indeed, childhood obesity is one of Dr. Fielding's greatest concerns. In an article that appeared shortly before Dr. Jerome Adams was sworn in as United States surgeon general in September 2017, Dr. Fielding urged Dr. Adams to use his public megaphone to help Americans who suffer from obesity and related health problems. He wrote, "[M]ore than one-third (35.7 percent) of adults in the [United States] are considered obese; more than 1 in 20 (6.3 percent) have extreme obesity. The Centers for Disease Control and Prevention note that about 17 percent of children ages two to nineteen are obese. Obesity affects about 12.7 million children and adolescents nationwide."[19]

Obesity has put us in the grip of a diabetes epidemic that threatens the lives of millions of Americans.[20] Dr. Fielding sounded the alarm in a 2017 *U.S. News and World Report* article in which he noted that 85.2 percent of people with type 2 diabetes are overweight or obese, and that people with diabetes have twice the risk of death compared to others of the same age. In total, he said, about 208,000 youths under twenty have type 2 diabetes. Tragically, these young people are "increasing their lifetime susceptibility to heart attacks, strokes, kidney failure, amputations, and blindness."[21]

Particularly frustrating to Dr. Fielding is that type 2 diabetes can be prevented. "Most Americans should be able to stave off type 2 diabetes by maintaining healthy weight through good diet, exercising regularly, and monitoring health through regular doctor visits."[22]

Complex roots of obesity and its intergenerational aspect

As Dr. Fielding writes in a report of the Los Angeles County Department of Public Health, the causes of obesity are complex, rooted in "an interactive mix of biological, behavioral, environmental, and socioeconomic factors." He notes that "prevalence differs greatly by race/ethnicity" and that "economic hardship is one of the major underlying factors contributing to the obesity epidemic."[23] Low-income areas often lack full-service grocery stores with affordable, healthy foods, and safe outdoor play spaces are also scarce.[24] Moreover, the report observes, such families do not always get the medical attention they need to identify preventable problems that can adversely affect their mental, physical, and social health.

This confluence of factors frequently leads to childhood obesity. Unfortunately, being overweight or obese early in life is a "bad portent," Dr. Fielding says. "It greatly increases your risk of having the same problem when you're older. If you're obese as a child, then you're four or five times more likely to be obese as an adult."[25]

Even worse news, Dr. Fielding stresses that obesity is intergenerational. "If you have an obese mother who gives birth to a child, when that child becomes an adult, he or she is more likely to become obese."[26] This could be for a number of reasons, including genetics, learning poor habits that get passed on to one's own children, or seeing being overweight as the accepted norm. "One's peer network, one's family, is important, and what people see as normal really does affect how they feel about themselves. So if everybody in your family is obese, you probably are not going to be as sensitive to it as somebody who comes from a family that generally has a lower level of body fat," Dr. Fielding points out.[27]

Today's sedentary lifestyles

Today's obesity epidemic is correlated with the inactive lives so many Americans lead. "I think the sedentary lifestyle is a problem," Dr. Fielding says. "We talk about physical activity as if it's separate from the rest of your life, something you do differently at a specific time you carve out. But we need to integrate physical activity into our daily lives, not just set aside special time for it."[28]

A perfect storm of circumstances has diverted far too many children from a healthy future. These include the following:

Undervaluing physical activity in schools: Schools face tremendous pressures today in allocating scarce resources of time and money. Too often, they cut back significantly on recess and physical education in order to spend more time on academics. State education authorities frequently ignore the mountains of evidence showing that active students do better academically and fail to fulfill their responsibility to set kids on a healthy path in life.[29] The need for more physical education in schools is of central concern to this book, and readers will learn more about this in the pages that follow.

Urban living and safety: Parents are understandably concerned about the safety of their children in urban environments. In cities, this often means taking public transportation to school rather than walking or biking—and playing indoors rather than risking unsafe parks and playgrounds.[30] Nor are walking and biking good options in heavily trafficked areas, which often lack sidewalks. Whatever the reasons, it is striking that whereas 40 percent of US schoolchildren walked or rode their bikes to school in 1969, only about 13 percent did so by 2001.[31]

High cost of recreational sports: Unaffordable fees for memberships and equipment make sports too expensive for many families. As children get older and progress in sports, travel teams are priced beyond the means of many.[32] Even school-based sports teams cost an average of $381 per year for each student, and although there may be other factors in play, 67 percent of teens in low-income families do not participate in school sports.[33] This is particularly troubling when one considers that obesity is more prevalent among low-income children.[34] Therefore, we have a situation where some of the children who most need physical activity have less access to it than children of higher income families do.

Movement-minimizing modern conveniences: We think of elevators, escalators, and moving walkways as good things. And they are, when you have heavy luggage or a meeting in a skyscraper. However, they have also reduced the need to walk and climb stairs. Similarly, other conveniences are blessings in one context and curses in another. For instance, air-conditioning causes us to want to remain indoors, and we'd often rather hop in our cars than walk ten minutes to a nearby store. All these modern conveniences mean we move less in our everyday lives—so it's even more important for kids to be active in school.

Hurried lives: Famous British economist John Maynard Keynes predicted in 1930 that technology and the growth of capital would permit us to work only about fifteen hours a week by about this time.[35] Things have not turned out that way, and the average hours worked in the United States are significantly longer than in most other industrialized countries.[36] While more leisure would not necessarily translate into healthier behaviors, many hurried families—especially when both parents work— prefer to save time by piling kids into the car or onto a bus rather than walk to a destination. It can also be quicker to cook high-calorie processed foods or to eat unhealthy fast food than to prepare a balanced meal.

Screen-focused entertainment: With a vast number of 24-7 entertainment choices and televisions that are five feet across, it is tempting for kids to become couch potatoes. Video games, on screens large and small, and social media browsing are more enticing to many kids than going outside to play actively. According to a 2015 report by Common Sense Media, tweens age eight to twelve and teens age thirteen to eighteen spend an alarming six and nine hours, respectively, looking at screens every day, and this excludes time spent using media for school or homework![37] Teens become absorbed in social media in their spare time instead of in activities that keep them moving. Tired and busy parents are often reluctant to limit screen time because it keeps the kids happily occupied.

Clearly, a broad range of factors contribute to today's inactivity epidemic. These factors, if not addressed, will only further the sedentary trends we are seeing in our children. "The research results are in," Dr. Fielding writes in *U.S. News and World Report*, "and they confirm that the newest generation of young people is in trouble. Post-millennials don't exercise, and that is the pathway to chronic diseases and lowered life expectancy," as well as to soaring health-care expenditures. Generally speaking, the older people get, the more sedentary they become. But shockingly, a research study to which Dr. Fielding refers in the article found that "19-year-olds showed the same amount of inactivity as 60-year-olds."[38]

This is disturbing not only because of the relationship between inactivity, becoming overweight, and the multiple health problems that can follow, from heart disease to diabetes, but also because, as Dr. Fielding says, "Physical activity improves mental health, improves how you approach things. It's a very common therapy for depression. And there is evidence that it improves cognitive performance."[39] I will explore these benefits at greater length later in the book.

Dr. Fielding is justifiably proud of what the L.A. County Department of Public Health did on his watch to combat obesity and promote physical activity. Among other initiatives, the department advocated for more physical education teachers at public schools; secured funding to pay for the police to be present in unsafe parks so that people could go out at night and stay active; and launched a "Choose Health LA" campaign to encourage people to make better choices in what they eat, even at fast-food restaurants.

Financial costs of inactivity

We tend to focus on the health consequences of inactivity, but the financial costs are enormous as well. Researchers in the Global Obesity Prevention Center at Johns Hopkins University recently predicted the savings that might accrue over a lifetime at different levels of childhood fitness. They found that a modest increase in the percentage of elementary school children who participate in twenty-five minutes of physical activity three times a week—from 32 percent to 50 percent—would save $21.9 billion in medical expenses and lost wages over the course of their lifetimes.[40] The same team at Johns Hopkins calculated that an overweight individual's lifetime medical expenses related to his or her excess weight average $62,331, and lost wages around $93,100, roughly double the costs for a person of healthy weight[41]—and enough money to put a kid through college or make a down payment on a house.

Clearly, to give children a financial boost in life, one great option is to help them develop good fitness habits and maintain a normal weight. But on a macro level, just think of all the wonderful ways we now, and they later on, could spend the money that currently goes to medical care for preventable diseases arising from inactivity and obesity. "There's a high opportunity cost for what we are spending on sickness care," notes Dr. Fielding. "There are a lot of things we could invest the potential savings in that would have a greater impact on our collective health and the huge health disparities. Better investing these savings could help reduce poverty, or homelessness, and improve educational attainment. In short, there are lots of ways to better invest our money than in more sickness care."[42]

A district student medical director's perspective

Like Dr. Fielding, Dr. Kimberly Uyeda began her career as a pediatrician before deciding to go into public health. For the past fourteen years, she has combined her expertise in pediatrics with a broader public health perspective as student medical services director of the Los

Angeles Unified School District (LAUSD). During this time, she says she has seen a "big push within the district and with our county public health system to make inroads into some of the root causes of obesity, causes [that] are deeply rooted in poverty, food insecurity, lack of open spaces, and more. I do think we've gotten a better sense of some of the multifactorial things that have to happen in order for us to see changes on the childhood obesity front and subsequently on the adult diseases front."[43]

Dr. Uyeda believes the school district has made great strides where nutrition is concerned, giving kids more healthy options in school meal programs as well as tweaking meal options to make healthy choices more attractive. For instance, in order for schools to be paid by the federal government for meals served to low-income children (the vast majority of those in the LAUSD),[44] cafeteria workers have to offer complete meals, with fruits and vegetables on each child's plate. But they cannot force kids to eat the food, and much food can go to waste. Then it was discovered that kids didn't like the whole pieces of fruit in their school meals; when fruit was cut up, they'd eat it.

Dr. Uyeda helped develop a highly successful five-week model program for seventh graders in the LAUSD, called SNaX (Students for Nutrition and eXercise), which deployed this kind of strategy and included peer-to-peer social marketing as well as an awareness campaign about the need for more physical activity. Participating students were given pedometers and instructions about exercises that could be done safely at home, such as dancing and jumping jacks, and at school. The results were very encouraging, with obese children in the program losing about nine pounds before they entered high school.[45]

The SNaX program was small, piloted in only five schools. But it shows what can be done with a relatively simple yet cost-effective (twenty-three cents per student per day)[46] intervention involving education and peer support, and it suggests a significant spillover effect in student homes as students shared what they learned with family members.

Thanks to changes made in recent years, Dr. Uyeda attests "you can go into any of our schools and find that our meals are appropriate and very healthy. We do have to have students eat the food, so we can't just serve kale all the time! But I would say that kids have really good meal choices in our schools, and some kids have three meals a day there."[47]

While Dr. Uyeda is pleased by the progress made on the nutrition front, she acknowledges that children "don't always have the same opportunity for physical activity. Our families who live in dense urban settings do not have the opportunity to recreate outside of school, especially if they do not live near a park."[48] Dr. Uyeda's observation further underscores the critical need for more physical education in schools and the kind of physical education that actually involves a high level of movement.

In the next chapter, we will learn more about the deadly duo of obesity and inactivity from one of the country's great pioneers in preventive medicine.

Crucial takeaways

- Obesity and inactivity pose a huge public health threat.
- A perfect storm of circumstances has led to today's sedentary lifestyles. We are much less active than our forebears were.
- The financial costs of inactivity to individuals and to society as a whole are as striking as the cost to our good health.
- The huge amount of money spent on health care resulting from obesity and inactivity could be redeployed to solve other societal problems that are major determinants of ill health.
- Schools have made considerable progress in providing more nutritious meals to students, but they have not promoted physical activity as effectively.
- When it comes to our commitment to fitness, we are overlooking the clear and undisputed lessons of history.

2

DEADLY DUO: INACTIVITY AND OBESITY

Dr. Kenneth Cooper certainly looks like a man who practices what he preaches. At eighty-seven years old, his lean frame would do credit to someone a quarter of his age, as befits a life-long exerciser. It is not surprising that a physician with a worldwide reputation as "the Father of Aerobics" should be concerned with fitness, but Dr. Cooper's commitment to fitness stems from a personal health crisis that occurred as a young man. He had been a competitive athlete in high school and college, playing basketball and running track, and earned a scholarship to the University of Oklahoma as a long-distance runner. But upon entering the University of Oklahoma College of Medicine in 1952 and during his subsequent internship, the stress of long hours and sleep deprivation (not to mention the culinary delights of a new marriage) caused him to overeat and to abandon the fitness regimen he had followed in college. As a result, he gained forty pounds, developed prediabetes, and became borderline hypertensive.

A frightening wake-up call

One day in 1960, the overweight twenty-nine-year-old had a cardiac event that was to shape the course of his life. While water-skiing for the first time in eight years, he developed a racing heart, accompanied by nausea and light-headedness, which sent him to the emergency room as soon as he got back to shore. He was sure he had had a heart attack. Mercifully, an extensive physical evaluation did not reveal anything structurally wrong with his heart, but in his out-of-shape and overweight state, he had experienced an episode of paroxysmal atrial tachycardia (PAT), a rapid heartbeat that occurs without warning. Although PAT is usually benign, this frightening episode spurred Dr. Cooper to lose the weight he gained within six months and to improve his fitness, even running the Boston Marathon. As a result, he lowered his blood pressure, moved out of the prediabetes stage, and noticed he also felt significantly better all around, not only physically but also with a more positive mental outlook.

He also charted a new course for his career: preventive medicine. In the 1960s, preventive medicine was called "the Cinderella of the medical profession," according to Dr. Cooper, "because there was no profit in health, only in disease."[1] However, he knew from his own personal health crisis as well as from his father's work as a periodontist that this was where he could have the greatest impact, preventing disease before it happened rather than going into primary care, "which could be associated with too much care too late."[2]

But first Dr. Cooper had a commitment to fulfill. After medical school and his internship, he earned a master's degree from Harvard's School of Public Health on a military scholarship. This required Dr. Cooper to give back in military service, and he ended up spending thirteen years in the US military, most notably as a flight surgeon and director of the USAF Aerospace Medical Laboratory in San Antonio, Texas. While aspiring one day to become an astronaut himself, he prepared others to go into space and developed a program to help them stay active and avoid unhealthy deconditioning in flight. He also did extensive research, working with twenty-seven thousand men and women at five air force bases, to develop a field test to assess astronaut candidate fitness before going into space. This resulted in the twelve-minute run, or "the Cooper test," which has been used by the NFL, World Cup soccer teams, police recruits, and many thousands of high school and college athletes. Dr. Cooper's work for the air force became the foundation of perhaps the most influential book about exercise in history, *Aerobics*,[3] which not only introduced a new word into the English language but also revolutionized how we thought about fitness. It has now been translated into forty-one languages as well as braille.

In the end, Dr. Cooper abandoned his dream of becoming an astronaut. He surmised it was likely to take several more years for him to be sent into space, and he had other important work he wanted to accomplish. So instead, he went into private practice, intent on exploring the relationship between cardiovascular fitness, health, and longevity. In 1970, he founded the Cooper Clinic in Dallas as well as its nonprofit research and education arm, the Cooper Institute. Forty-eight years later, Cooper Aerobics is home to the largest repository in the world of fitness data related to health, and it is recognized globally for its work spurring millions to lead longer, healthier lives. Among his other international endeavors, Dr. Cooper trained the Brazilian soccer team to a World Cup victory in 1970, and as a result, in Portuguese "coopering" is now one word for "jogging." In 2017, he opened a state-of-the-art health and wellness center in Nanjing, China, where physical education teachers, personal trainers, and doctors will learn about fitness as preventive medicine. Along with its economic advancement, China has also seen skyrocketing rates of obesity and diabetes.[4] Never one to think small, Dr. Cooper is determined to improve the health of China's 1.37 billion people.

Looming catastrophe

At home, Dr. Cooper has been a tireless combatant in the fight against childhood obesity and inactivity, which he says threaten the future health of the nation. According to the Cooper Institute, only 26.6 percent of six-to-twelve year olds and 39.3 percent of thirteen-to-seventeen-year-olds are active to a healthy level at least three times a week.[5] "Kids today are more overweight and less fit than at any other time in our history," Dr. Cooper says. "It takes teenagers today one to one and a half minutes longer to run a mile than their parents—if they can even make it that far."[6] As reported in a study presented to the American Heart Association in 2013, our children's cardiovascular endurance declined an average of 6 percent per decade between 1970–2000, meaning that children today are some 15 percent less heart-fit than their parents were.[7] Given that heart disease is the leading cause of death in the United States,[8] clearly their parents can't be very heart-fit to begin with, which makes this decline even more concerning.

The combination of obesity and inactivity is a deadly duo. "The lack of a balanced diet coupled with a lack of regular daily physical activity are increasingly leading to such debilitating conditions as heart disease, diabetes, weight gain, and depression, as well as reduced academic performance and school absenteeism," explains Dr. Cooper.[9] Conditions most commonly seen in adults in years past are now showing up in children. These include a type of fatty liver disease that can eventually cause permanent damage in the form of hepatitis and cirrhosis[10] as well as hypertension and type 2 diabetes.[11] "The unprecedented epidemic of childhood obesity and diabetes go hand in hand, and diabetes can result in kidney failure requiring dialysis and, at times, kidney transplants," Dr. Cooper warns.[12]

The United States is certainly not the only country facing a health crisis like this. On the contrary, it is virtually a worldwide problem.[13] However, as Dr. Cooper points out, some countries are tackling the threat head-on, determined to turn things around. China, for instance, calls the obesity epidemic among its children "the most fearful enemy to their health," Dr. Cooper reports. "Why do I go to China?" Dr. Cooper asks rhetorically. "Because they listen to me. They don't listen to me in the United States. It's really sad to say, but I've been talking to a blank wall here for years."[14]

Although we in this country have been slow to act, other countries are taking steps to address the acute dangers of obesity and inactivity. "One country I'm very proud of is France, because they have made a major effort to eliminate obesity," says Dr. Cooper. "Right now, their adults are about 18 percent obese, whereas we here in the United

States are at 35 percent. In addition, England is better than we are, at 28 percent. I also noticed [that] in Japan, they started a program several years ago having to do with measuring waist circumference. If corporations didn't meet the stipulated requirement, they would be fined. So as a result, there was a dramatic improvement in the obesity problem there. And in a city in Russia, when you stood in front of the subway token machine and did a certain number of squats, they gave you a free ticket. So there are definitely unique things that countries are doing around the world. However, it's sad how we are doing basically nothing in the United States to try [to] correct the situation. We're going to have a problem in the future that's going to blow your mind, I can assure you!"[15]

Inactivity as "the new smoking"

As noted in the last chapter, being overweight has many causes, ranging from genes, family income, and environment to other lifestyle factors and food choices. However, one thing is clear: If you don't burn off the calories you consume, you will gain weight. Exercise is not the whole answer to weight control, but it is an important component. Conversely, inactivity is a significant risk factor for becoming overweight or obese, and given how inactive children are today, we are setting them up for a host of serious health conditions and disorders. A 2010 study published in the *New England Journal of Medicine* found that childhood obesity more than doubles the risk of dying before age fifty-five.[16] Also disturbing is a recent report from the Centers for Disease Control that says the rates of twelve obesity-related cancers rose by 7 percent from 2005 to 2014. These obesity-related cancers constitute 40 percent of all cancers diagnosed in 2014.[17] While the science linking cancer to obesity is still evolving, there is consistent evidence that high amounts of body fat are associated with a number of cancers, including pancreatic, colorectal, kidney, and liver cancers.[18]

A World Health Organization (WHO) report is no less alarming. It contends that physical inactivity is now "the fourth leading risk factor for global mortality, behind high blood pressure, tobacco use, and high blood glucose." Moreover, the report notes, "Inactivity is estimated as being the principal cause for approximately 21 to 25 percent of breast and colon cancer burden, 27 percent of diabetes, and approximately 30 percent of ischemic heart disease burden" around the world.[19]

While these figures concern adults, they are still very troubling for children. Inactivity begins in childhood, and inactive adults seem to pass their sedentary lifestyles on to the next generation.[20] If you tend to be sedentary, chances are high that your kids will be too. In fact, parents who are inactive are 5.8 times more likely to have inactive children.[21] Unfortunately, despite all we know about the life-threatening danger of inactivity, our society doesn't do nearly enough to get kids moving.

It is worth saying that while inactivity is certainly related to obesity, inactive children of normal weight are still at risk.[22] Inactivity itself, even when individuals are not overweight, is dangerous. Conversely, overweight people who remain active reduce their risk factors. A 2012 study by researchers at the National Institutes of Health found that leisure-time physical activity is associated with gains of as much as 4.5 years in life expectancy, even at relatively low levels of activity and regardless of body weight. Stephen Moore, PhD, the study's lead author, reports the following: "Regular exercise extended the lives in every group that we examined in our study—normal weight, overweight, or obese."[23]

Yet Dr. Cooper says that one of the most surprising and dramatic facts he's learned in sixty-two years of medical practice is how little exercise is necessary to reap health benefits. "I always thought in the early years that you had to be aerobically fit, getting what we call 'the training effect' from exercise, to have any benefit. But the studies of our own research showed it wasn't necessary to reach that high level of fitness. Just avoiding inactivity—that is, getting thirty minutes of sustained or collective activity most days per week—could reduce deaths of all causes by 58 percent and increase life expectancy by six years."[24]

Once again, Dr. Cooper is speaking here of adults. Children need more exercise. For an adult, the recommended amount of physical activity is 150 minutes of moderate exertion, like brisk walking, a week—or just a little over twenty minutes a day.[25] For children, it's an hour of moderate-to-vigorous activity *on a daily basis.*[26] As you might expect, children need more exercise because they are growing. If they don't get sufficient exercise, Dr. Cooper explains, "They're going to grow with muscles laden with fat, and that's why the majority will be obese by thirty-five years of age. They need to exercise more to burn up this fat, and this must be paired with controlled diet as well. And they need to develop strong bones, and that occurs with weight-bearing exercise."[27]

According to the Aspen Institute, children who do not get sufficient exercise are not only prone to gaining weight but also lose more days at school and have less academic success. "They're twice as likely to be obese as adults. They'll earn less at work, have higher health-care costs, and take extra sick days. Physical inactivity impairs quality of life [and] drains economies …"[28]

There are implications for our military preparedness as well, which is not surprising in a country where the percentage of children with obesity has more than tripled since the 1970s.[29] Dr. Cooper notes, "At least 60 to 70 percent of the people trying to enter the military cannot qualify because of academic ability, drugs, obesity, or levels of fitness. Ten percent of active duty personnel are not qualified for deployment due to obesity and injuries. As a result, [the armed services] are changing their fitness requirements."[30]

According to the *2016 United States Report Card for Physical Activity in Children and Youth*, only 42.5 percent of six- to eleven-year-olds, 7.5 percent of twelve- to fifteen-year-olds, and 5 percent of sixteen- to nineteen-year-olds get sixty minutes of physical activity even five days a week.[31] This is, of course, two days short per week of the recommended minimum for good health. Adults do somewhat better; about 44 percent of them are within their healthy activity range.[32] Therefore, the inactivity plague disproportionately affects our youth and is nothing short of a ticking time bomb. Its effects, if we don't change course, will be devastating in the future. *The Lancet*, a renowned British medical journal, has published a series of articles on physical inactivity and calls it a "global pandemic" responsible for an estimated 5.3 million deaths a year.[33] Indeed, this prestigious journal says that not moving enough can be as detrimental to one's health as smoking.[34]

Measuring childhood fitness: the FitnessGram

For Dr. Cooper, his concern with childhood fitness is not only professional; it's personal. As the grandfather of five, he is passionate about children's health, and his nonprofit Cooper Institute has been a key agent of change in promoting physical activity for kids in schools. "I think PE should be a core subject," Dr. Cooper says. "I've been fighting for years to make it a core subject like reading, math, and writing."[35] This resonated with me, as I have been convinced for the past twenty years that we are shortchanging our children when we consider PE a curricular "extra" of little importance.

The Cooper Institute is probably best known for developing the FitnessGram, the first "student fitness report card," with the goal of improving school physical education programs and building awareness of children's fitness levels. Dr. Cooper strongly believes that just as students need to know how they're doing academically, they should also be aware of their fitness grades and understand the relationship between fitness and overall health. The FitnessGram, first introduced in 1982, assesses five basic components of fitness:[36]

> **Aerobic capacity:** This has to do with improving the body's oxygen consumption and is probably the most important aspect of fitness. Aerobic exercise (also called cardiovascular exercise) challenges your heart and lungs to work harder through continuous exercise that engages your large muscles, such as your legs. Examples include running, walking, and cycling. As you build cardiorespiratory endurance, your heart works

more efficiently to pump blood, and more oxygen reaches your muscles. This helps control blood pressure and cholesterol, also reducing the risk for several diseases, including type 2 diabetes, some cancers, and, of course, heart disease.

Muscle Strength: Muscular strength is the maximal force your muscles can exert in a single effort. Strong muscles enable us to do all kinds of things we need to do every day, such as lifting, pulling, and pushing—and to do so with less chance of injury. Weight-bearing exercise in particular, which includes anything done on your feet, helps build bone mass and is especially important for children. The greatest gains in bone mass occur just before and during puberty, so childhood is a critical time to get exercise.[37]

Muscle Endurance: Endurance has to do with how often you can repeat use of the same muscle. You can't really separate muscle endurance from muscle strength. Good endurance enables you to stay longer with performing repetitive tasks such as raking leaves, rowing, or loading a moving van.

Flexibility: This is about the range of motion of any joint in the body. Flexibility has a major impact on one's ability to perform all sorts of daily tasks and to improve other areas of fitness. Without flexibility, one also sacrifices agility and becomes more prone to injury.

Body Composition: Body composition is an important measure of fitness and health for everyone and concerns the percentage of fat in the body. Carrying too much fat affects all other aspects of fitness, as it reduces speed, endurance, and agility.

One unique aspect of the FitnessGram is the Healthy Fitness Zone[38] evaluation system. Fitness levels are classified based on a student's age and sex to provide a personalized health target. There are three categories for each test: Healthy Fitness Zone (HFZ), Needs Improvement, and Needs Improvement—Health Risk. The goal for all students is to place within the Healthy Fitness Zone for each test. Being in the HFZ means a student has sufficient fitness for good health. The Needs Improvement category alerts students that there is a potential for future health risks at current fitness levels. Finally, the Needs Improvement—Health Risk category indicates that there is a clear potential for future health problems and underscores a more urgent need to adopt healthy habits. These three categories provide a simple yet effective way to evaluate student fitness levels and have been instrumental in helping schools better track student performance and build more effective physical education programs.

As the educational assessment and reporting software portion of the Presidential Youth Fitness Program, a comprehensive school-based program that promotes health and regular physical activity for America's youth, the FitnessGram is used in schools across the United States as well as in a number of foreign countries—over twenty thousand schools and ten million students in total.[39] Its evidence-based comprehensive testing has been an invaluable tool in helping children track their fitness levels and learn the value of a physically active lifestyle. In addition, the data collected through FitnessGram enables schools to monitor trends and changes in student fitness over time, see how fitness correlates with attendance and academic achievement, develop better PE programs, and communicate more effectively on health and fitness issues with parents and children. Thanks to the FitnessGram, I can't think of any single organization that has had a more profound influence on childhood fitness than the Cooper Institute.

Dr. Cooper recalls working with Governor Rick Perry of Texas to implement the FitnessGram in state schools in the early 2000s. "We found the test results to be terrible, which we published in newspapers throughout Texas," Dr. Cooper says. "By the twelfth grade, fewer than 8 percent of both boys and girls could reach the Healthy Fitness

Zone. That shook up the state! The next year [2007–2008 school year], we tested 2.4 million kids in the state. Of those who were physically fit, there was a perfect correlation to academic achievement and absenteeism was way down. The impact exercise has on the growing brain is unparalleled. Increased exercise improves cardiovascular health, and that helps the brain function more efficiently and enhances its ability to learn."[40] The test also found that higher fitness levels were associated with fewer disciplinary incidents involving drugs, alcohol, violence, and truancy.[41] The FitnessGram became mandatory in Texas schools, as it is now in twelve other states.[42]

The FitnessGram is just one of many new tools that have been developed to measure and track fitness as well as to motivate individuals to strive harder. Years ago, fitness was generally defined as the ability to meet the physical demands of daily life without undue fatigue. Today, however, when so many people work at desks and automation has made many jobs and chores less physically demanding, this definition no longer works very well. It is striking to note that in 2000, only 23 percent of Americans worked in high-activity occupations, a 7 percent drop from 1950.[43] Conversely, the percentage of people working in low-activity occupations rose from about 23 percent to 41 percent in the same period.[44] Most of us can meet the physical demands of daily life without taxing our muscles or elevating our heart rates. Instead, physical fitness today is thought of more in terms of measurable components, both health and skill related.

Accordingly, there are scores of apps on the market, many of which are free, that will help record workouts, count calories, and log data about bike rides, walks, and runs to see how one is doing over time. There are also apps that provide a workout routine or motivate with music. The most important tool in my own fitness arsenal is a simple heart rate monitor that lets me find my "sweet spot" for an effective workout so that I am challenging myself but not overtraining. This involves identifying my maximum heart rate, then staying in that zone for a specific amount of time. Recommendations for maximum heart rate vary with age, and heart rate monitors make it much easier to get the right aerobic workout. A number of schools now use them when budgets permit, and they are a huge motivator for kids, allowing them to track their performance and see improvement. The profound impact of heart rate monitoring technology was clearly shown in a case study at a school in Illinois, which we will discuss later in the book.

Dr. Cooper's formula for health

In addition to monitoring a child's fitness levels, Dr. Cooper recommends parents work with their children to follow the 8-5-3-2-1-0 formula:[45]

- 8 hours of sleep a night
- 5 servings of fruits and vegetables each day
- 3 servings of low-fat dairy products daily
- 2 hours maximum of TV and computer use each day
- 1 hour of exercise a day
- 0 sugar-sweetened beverages

If we are committed to healthy eating and exercise, we can hope to live as long and vigorously as Dr. Cooper, who at eighty-seven still does thirty to thirty-five minutes on a stationary bike or two miles on the treadmill every day, followed by a circuit training routine with six machines for about ten to fifteen minutes. He says, "I exercise before my evening meal because exercise suppresses the appetite and stimulates the metabolism to be more active. It makes you thirsty but not hungry. So having children exercise before the heaviest meal of the day can help reduce their appetite and control their weight."[46] A 2013 study in Australia found that individuals who engaged in high-intensity exercise before eating had lower levels of a hormone, ghrelin, which stimulates appetite; and higher levels of blood lactate and blood sugar, which dull appetite.[47]

Prevention: a hopeful future

There's a lot of bad news in this chapter, but there is also much hope. Many diseases are preventable, and we do not have to accept the status quo. Dr. Cooper observes, "Seventy-six percent of diseases we have in America today are a result of lifestyle, and 45 percent of cancers can be prevented. We can now identify and predict cancers based on obesity, inactivity, use of tobacco in any form—even alcohol is related—and finally vitamin D deficiencies."[48]

If you're wondering whether it's beyond your child's—or your—reach to become fit, don't worry. As Dr. Cooper notes earlier in this chapter, the great news is that even a modest increase in physical activity reaps health benefits. You don't need to run a four-minute mile to achieve significant health improvements; just about any type of moderately intense movement counts so long as you do it for at least ten minutes at a time. Walking at a good clip, raking leaves, and jogging alongside a dog all count as exercise. Whatever works for your family will produce rewards so long as you meet the recommended minimum of two and a half hours a week for adults[49] and an hour a day for children and adolescents.[50] It doesn't have to be expensive.

So we have it within our power to turn things around, especially if we start early to teach good habits to our children. As Dr. Cooper says, "Obese children become obese adults. It is easier to maintain good health through proper exercise, diet, and emotional balance than to regain it once it is lost."[51]

Parents can have a positive impact on their children's development by modeling a healthy lifestyle through good nutritional and fitness choices, in addition to finding times to exercise together as a family—anything from taking a brisk walk to going for a bike ride or playing basketball at a neighborhood court. This is a great way to enjoy each other's company and to have fun together while enjoying the benefits of aerobic activity. Parents can also make room for more physical activity by reducing the amount of time children are allowed to spend in sedentary activities such as watching TV or sitting at the computer.

Dr. Cooper hopes his legacy will be seen as the impact he has had in fighting childhood obesity and inactivity. We can all strive to leave our children this legacy of good health.

Crucial takeaways

- Obesity and inactivity are a deadly duo. Unless the present situation changes, this may be the first generation in which children live shorter life spans than their parents.
- Ironically, one of the most dangerous activities in the world is to remain inactive. Inactivity has become known as "the new smoking."
- Exercise is medicine and can prevent many serious diseases. It is a well-established fact that exercise is one of the best things you can do for your health.
- Parents who model healthful choices for their children help their kids develop good habits early on.
- Many killer diseases are preventable. This is great news! Still better, only a modest increase in activity levels can bring about tremendous health and financial benefits.
- With greater awareness of the dangers of inactivity and the benefits of exercise, we can make decisions that will improve our children's health for a lifetime.

3

EXERCISE: "MIRACLE-GRO FOR THE BRAIN"

A junior in high school has trouble learning all the Spanish vocabulary words she needs to know for her SAT II subject test. What can she do to boost her score?

An eighth grader leads a chaotic life. He is clearly intelligent and can focus well when something really catches his attention. However, he generally runs late, rarely turns a paper in on time, and spaces out in class. What can be done to mitigate these classic signs of ADHD?

A boy's parents are going through a divorce, and the emotional strain is affecting his academic work. He is anxious and sad, and he can't concentrate. What would help boost his spirits?

****

If you guessed "exercise" as the answer to the above questions, you get an A grade. Most people are familiar with the positive effects of exercise on one's overall physical health, but in recent years, more and more evidence has accumulated about its profound cognitive and mental health benefits. As the brain is part of the human body, it should come as no surprise that exercise is just as capable of affecting our minds as it is of strengthening our cardiovascular systems.

Perhaps no one has shed more light on the exercise-brain connection than Dr. John Ratey, the eminent Harvard psychiatrist and best-selling author of *Spark: The Revolutionary New Science of Exercise and the Brain.*

John Ratey grew up in the steel town of Beaver Falls in western Pennsylvania, part of the country he calls "football central," where such gridiron luminaries as Joe Namath, Tony Dorsett, and Mike Ditka came from. Afflicted with flat feet, he didn't make it very far in football and gravitated toward basketball, tennis, and squash instead. He excelled at tennis, winning an athletic scholarship to Colgate University, but didn't think too much about exercise and health in those days. "I grew up in an area where you were doing sports all the time, and it was just in my blood," Dr. Ratey says. "The real light bulb about exercise didn't go off until I was in medical school and the new antidepressants had just come into use. We called them 'miracle drugs.' About this time, I heard about a study of people who were hospitalized for depression in Norway. They'd be offered either one of the new antidepressants or an exercise program, and they found both treatments produced the same results. That really changed how I looked at exercise."[1]

Dr. Ratey went on to become a psychiatrist and had another epiphany when he was serving as Harvard's director of residency and medical study training. He recalls: "I was at a cocktail party discussing attention deficit disorder with a group of people, one of whom asked if he could come see me in my office later. This man was one of those 'great minds.' He held faculty positions at both Harvard and MIT and had won a MacArthur Fellowship. He had written many books and was an esteemed scholar. He was also a serious marathoner, but he had to stop running when his right knee got balky. He then found he became depressed and showed symptoms of ADD. I treated him with some medicine, helped him, and stayed with him, and eventually he got back to running. At that point, he stopped the medicine and his symptoms disappeared. He self-treated with exercise."[2]

From then on, Dr. Ratey began to track the literature on exercise and the brain very closely. At the time, it was meager. He recollects: "In the mid-1990s, there were a bunch of studies from UC Irvine showing what exercise did to prevent the onset of Alzheimer's disease, first in mice and then in people. Then it exploded! Neuroscientists began to recognize that exercise was really, really important."[3]

While maintaining his clinical practice, Dr. Ratey wrote three books on attention deficit disorder with his former student Dr. Edward Hallowell, including *Driven to Distraction*, which has sold over two and a half million copies since it was first published in 1994 and is considered the bible on the subject. "In our books," Dr. Ratey says, "we always talk about how exercise is one of the key ways in which you can help yourself, because we know what it does in the brain."[4]

Learning from Naperville Central High School

In 2008, Dr. Ratey wrote *Spark: The Revolutionary New Science of Exercise and the Brain*. Just as Dr. Kenneth Cooper's *Aerobics* transformed the way people think about exercise and heart health, so *Spark* has had an enormous effect on the way people regard exercise and the brain.[5] The inspiration for the book was, in part, a remarkable visit Dr. Ratey had to Naperville Central High School near Chicago. "I heard about this school in Naperville, and it blew me away," he says. "Apparently, just 3 percent of their kids were overweight, when the average in America was 33 percent. Moreover, the eighth graders in the Naperville School District 203 had taken an international science and math test and came in first in science and sixth in math in the world!"[6]

This was far ahead of the rankings of the United States as a whole, eighteenth and nineteenth in the two subjects, highlighting the sharp performance divide between Naperville and the rest of the country. Granted, Naperville was an affluent suburb, but there were many wealthy suburbs in the nation with significantly higher per student spending and Naperville was leaving most of them in the dust academically. Something must be different about this school, and John

Ratey wanted to know what it was. "This got me on an airplane pretty quickly," he recalls.[7]

Dr. Ratey discovered that physical educators in Naperville didn't just teach the kids how to play sports, which often means a lot of inactivity when kids are waiting for their turn. Instead, they taught their students a fit lifestyle and focused on students doing their personal best so they could still succeed in class even if they weren't especially athletic. "The underlying philosophy," Dr. Ratey writes in *Spark*, "is that if physical education class can be used to instruct kids how to monitor and maintain their own health and fitness, then the lessons they learn will serve them for life. And probably a longer and happier life at that."[8] A key ingredient in Naperville's program was the use of heart rate monitors to provide students with immediate feedback on their performance and output. This allowed for more personalized and efficient workouts for each student.

Dr. Ratey was particularly struck by a program at Naperville Central High School called Zero Hour. The students in the program were those who needed to improve their reading comprehension, and they came in at "zero hour," before school started, to get significant aerobic exercise, running track close to their maximum heart rates. It turns out these students did 7 percent better on their reading comprehension than students who took the standard PE class. And those who took their literacy class right after PE in the morning did better than those who took it toward the end of the school day.[9] In light of these powerful results, today counselors at Naperville try to schedule PE at times that will benefit students most, before their hardest classes. Moreover, Zero Hour has morphed into Learning Readiness Physical Education, an approach to PE and learning that is now embedded in the curriculum and has been adapted as a statewide standard.

Dr. Ratey's first meeting with Phil Lawler and Paul Zientarski, Naperville's pioneering physical educators, lasted about four hours. "It was just an amazing meeting," says Dr. Ratey. "These were PE teachers who figured things out and changed the culture at their school but didn't know why their program worked so well. I was able to provide the 'why.'"[10]

Why exercise has such a powerful effect on learning

As Dr. Ratey explains in *Spark*, exercise releases a cascade of neurochemicals and growth factors that bolster the brain's infrastructure, including BDNF—brain-derived neurotrophic factor—which Dr. Ratey calls "Miracle-Gro for the brain." As a result, alertness, attention, and motivation all grow—and learning potential does too. Dr. Ratey puts it simply: "Exercise improves learning on three levels. It optimizes your mind-set to improve alertness, attention, and motivation. It prepares and encourages nerve cells to bind to one another, which helps log new information at the cellular level. And it leads to the development of new nerve cells in the hippocampus, the area of the brain responsible for many aspects of learning and memory. Exercise makes all our brain systems work better."[11]

Dr. Ratey writes that there are good reasons rooted in humankind's distant past for this: "Learning and memory evolved in concert with the motor functions that allowed our ancestors to track down food, so as far as our brains are concerned, if we're not moving, there's no real need to learn anything."[12] He is also excited about what new research is showing. "We found out, maybe three years ago," Dr. Ratey says, "that when a cell fires and releases BDNF, it sends a feedback loop back to the genes of the presynaptic neuron, or the firing nerve cell, to turn on machinery to make more BDNF. It's self-generating. The more you use it, the more BDNF you get. The more 'Miracle-Gro' you get. This is really amazing."[13]

Exploring all the science behind why exercise is so beneficial is beyond the scope of this book, but it is substantial and growing. Readers who would like to dig deeper into the biological effects of exercise will not find a better place to start than John Ratey's *Spark*, a highly readable and informative book. I would also refer you to *Healthy Brain, Happy*

Life,[14] by neuroscientist Dr. Wendy Suzuki. Part personal memoir, Dr. Suzuki's book describes how she improved her own life through her knowledge of the brain-body connection and gives readers "brain hacks" to augment their brainpower. Both are fascinating books in which Drs. Ratey and Suzuki describe the brain as a dynamic organ whose cells and circuitry change throughout our lives. They clearly explain how exercise can help us tap into the brain's extraordinary powers, and I can't recommend these books highly enough.

New research on exercise and learning

More and more evidence continues to accumulate that exercise helps children become better learners and that it helps all of us grow and maintain our cognitive capacity. In an interview with psychologist Rick Hanson, Dr. Ratey underscores the massive evidence to this effect: "We increase our use of brain cells in exercise, more than we do in any other human activity. The studies are clear: sixteen hundred papers point to a positive effect of exercise improving cognitive capacity."[15]

Two of the most active scholars in this field are Professors Charles Hillman of Northeastern University and Darla Castelli of the University of Texas at Austin. Both have devoted their careers to studying the effects of physical activity on cognitive performance and have collaborated together and with others on a number of published studies, including:

> *Pediatrics*: In a randomized controlled 2014 study published in the official journal of the American Academy of Pediatrics, elementary school children who got at least sixty minutes of moderate to vigorous physical activity after school improved their memory, attention, and multitasking skills.[16] Professor Hillman called the results of the study "the hardest evidence we have available that time spent in physical activities, which would include physical education and recess, not only doesn't detract from academic goals, but it might [also] enhance academic performance."[17]

Journal of Teaching in Physical Education: An article based on a 2014 study supports the results of Naperville's Zero Hour program. Eighth graders who engaged in vigorous physical exercise thirty minutes before a math test performed 11–22 percent better than those who did not.[18] It appears that even short bouts of exercise prior to testing help students achieve better grades.

Neuroscience: A study published in this international journal found that even moderate exercise in the form of walking was beneficial for cognitive function in a series of tasks given to nine-year-old girls. "They had a higher rate of accuracy, especially when the task was more difficult," Professor Hillman said. He also noted that they were "better able to allocate attentional resources."[19]

The *Neuroscience* study would suggest that exercise can help the inattentive child, and indeed there is abundant research that this is the case. A 2014 article in *The Journal of Pediatrics* discusses a study that found that after just twenty minutes of exercise, "both children with ADHD and healthy match control children exhibited greater response accuracy and stimulus-related processing … In addition, greater performance in the areas of reading and arithmetic were observed following exercise in both groups."[20]

Effects of exercise on mental and emotional well-being

Exercise can also have profound effects on our emotional and mental health. According to the Mayo Clinic, when exercise stimulates the production of endorphins, the brain's feel-good neurotransmitters, it "can increase self-confidence, it can relax you, and it can lower the symptoms associated with mild depression and anxiety. Exercise can also improve your sleep, which is often disrupted by stress, depression, and anxiety."[21] No one treatment works for everyone, but exercise can be every bit as therapeutic as medications in alleviating some forms of anxiety and depression.

Dr. Nadine Burke Harris, author of *The Deepest Well: Healing the Long-Term Effects of Childhood Adversity*,[22] names exercise as one of the six key components to address the biology of toxic stress. She tells the *New York Times*, "[W]hen you exercise, it helps to metabolize stress hormones and releases other hormones that counteract effects of stress and also support cardiovascular health and reduce chronic inflammation."[23]

Along the same lines, a recent study by researchers at George Mason University discovered that college students had more positive social interactions and accomplished more of the goals they set themselves on days when they exercise. However, the study did not show that feeling better one day makes you want to get out and exercise the next. According to the study's lead author, "When we become depressed or whatever it is we're going through, we say to ourselves that we'll get out when we feel better. Unfortunately, what we also see is that we do not feel better until we get out."[24] Therefore, the life lesson here (as I suggest in my introduction to this book) is that it pays to develop the habit of exercising regularly to boost your mood.

In today's age of social media, when children spend hours alone with their screens, Dr. Ratey sees the social aspect of exercise and sport as crucial to their development. "When you talk about where our world is going, and where our kids are going, the lack of socialization is going to be really, really important. It's a huge problem now, but it's going to be a massive problem as we get into artificial intelligence and people just cannot be as involved with others. One of the things that happens when you get active is that you decrease your loneliness, so this is another reason sports and exercise are so important."[25] It is perhaps no coincidence, Dr. Ratey thinks, that the United Kingdom's undersecretary for sport and civil society, Tracey Crouch, was recently charged with addressing the nation's epidemic of loneliness.[26]

Autism and exercise: a personal story

Dr. Ratey and other experts also advocate exercise for children with autism, a condition that afflicts one in every forty-one children in the United States.[27] According to the Autism Research Institute, exercise is one of the best therapies for individuals with autism: "Studies have shown that vigorous or strenuous exercise is associated with decreases in stereotypic (self-stimulatory) behaviors, hyperactivity, aggression, self-injury, and destructiveness."[28]

I would like to share a personal perspective with you. Our eldest son, Willie, has autism. At thirty years old, he is thriving in a residential program, working at Home Depot, and painting wonderful landscapes, mostly focused on sea life. He has an incredible sense of color. While he's on a much better track now, for many years we struggled quite intensely with his behavioral issues and defiance. We were also concerned about his weight, which soared to 220 pounds—a lot even for a six-footer like Willie. Although I often encouraged him to work out with me, it wasn't until he met Greg Simpson, the kind but definitely no-nonsense leader of my son's care team, that he actually started to get the exercise he so badly needed. Greg was not someone Willie wanted to cross, so when he encouraged him to get on the treadmill, Willie complied. That was four years ago. Today, Willie has ramped up his workout to two hours a day, runs regularly, and is an eager participant in local races. The results have been tremendous. Not only did Willie lose forty pounds, but also his overall attitude has changed dramatically. He is significantly less defiant in his behavior and much more positive in his outlook. In our experience, exercise has been a far more effective therapy than all the others we tried. Some of them worked for a little while, but none of them has produced the kind of long-term change in Willie that exercise has brought about.

Educating the student body

Much of the research I have mentioned concerning fitness and learning is nicely summed up in a 2013 report from the Institute of Medicine, titled *Educating the Student Body: Taking Physical Activity and Physical Education to School.* Noting the alarming increase in the prevalence of noncommunicable diseases such as obesity, many of which begin in childhood, as well as the cognitive benefits of PE, the report calls for a "whole-of-school" approach to providing physical activity. This includes increasing physical activity not only in PE classes and recess, but also through dedicated classroom physical activity time and in opportunities before and after school. The report recommends that the Department of Education designate physical education as a core subject, and it contains the following key messages concerning the positive impact of physical activity on learning:

- Evidence suggests that increasing physical activity and physical fitness may improve academic performance and that time in the school day dedicated to recess, physical education class, and physical activity in the classroom may also facilitate academic performance.

- Available evidence suggests that mathematics and reading are the academic topics most influenced by physical activity. These topics depend on efficient and effective executive function, which has been linked to physical activity and physical fitness. [Executive function is a group of mental skills that help us to organize and plan.]

- Executive function and brain health underlie academic performance. Basic cognitive functions related to attention and memory facilitate learning, and these functions are enhanced by physical activity and higher aerobic fitness.

- Single sessions of and long-term participation in physical activity improve cognitive performance and brain health. Children who participate in vigorous or moderate-intensity physical activity benefit the most.

- Given the importance of time on task to learning, students should be provided with frequent physical activity breaks that are developmentally appropriate.
- Although presently understudied, physically active lessons offered in the classroom may increase time on task and attention to task in the classroom setting.[29]

The pool of research findings highlighting the multiple benefits of physical activity is continually growing, thanks to the work of John Ratey, Darla Castelli, Charles Hillman, Wendy Suzuki, and many, many others. And although we are vastly more sedentary than we should be for optimal health, Dr. Ratey is pleased that a fit lifestyle is becoming cooler, at least among adults: "If you look at TV commercials, so many of them are about exercise, working out, or getting outdoors … It's a part of things. It never was there before. Advertisers are trying to entice people not just with a good-looking guy or girl necessarily, but with someone who's getting fit. I think there has been so much of this in the media that it's helping to turn the tide a bit. People are saying 'Well, I've got to get my Fitbit on!'"[30]

Alas, where we are failing dismally (with some wonderful exceptions) is in summoning the will to ensure physical fitness is a priority in schools. This is why programs like the one in Naperville are so critically important; they demonstrate what dedicated physical educators can achieve—academically as well as in other areas of student well-being—when their school districts support them. This is where true change must take place so that schools have the time and budget resources necessary to give all children a healthy start in life through effective fitness education. We can make no better investment in their future.

In the next chapter, I'll address the state of PE in America today with the help of one of the leading experts in the field.

Crucial takeaways

- The brain is a dynamic organ whose cells and circuitry change throughout our lives.
- Exercise is one of the primary ways in which we grow our cognitive capacity.
- A great many studies show that fit kids are better learners.
- Powerful academic benefits come from a purposeful and focused physical education program.
- Physical activity also has positive effects on children's emotional and mental health.
- School districts must allocate the time and budget resources necessary to give children a healthy start in life through fitness education.

4

REPORT CARD: THE STATE OF PHYSICAL EDUCATION IN AMERICAN SCHOOLS TODAY

A country is as strong, really, as its citizens, and I think that mental and physical health, mental and physical vigor, go hand in hand.[1]

—John F. Kennedy

When people think of President Kennedy, the first thing that usually comes to mind is the tragedy of his assassination, followed closely, perhaps, by the Cuban Missile Crisis. Most people have forgotten that he was a passionate advocate for physical fitness for all Americans, and—as the quotation above shows—he clearly recognized the connection between fitness and intellectual attainment as well as emotional well-being. He thought that youth fitness was a measure of the vitality of the nation and wrote as president-elect in *Sports Illustrated*, "The physical fitness of our citizens is a vital prerequisite to America's realization of its full potential as a nation, and to the opportunity of each individual citizen to make full and fruitful use of his capacities."[2] I venture to say he would be horrified by the state of physical education in schools today, where PE has become little more than an afterthought in many districts.

Here are the disturbing facts according to the Presidential Youth Fitness Program:[3]

- Only six US states require physical education in all grades K–12.
- Not a single state follows the national recommendations for physical education time at all levels: 150 minutes/week (30 minutes/day) for elementary school students and 225 minutes/week (45 minutes/day) for middle and high school students.
- As I mentioned in my introduction, the median school budget for physical education is $764. In a school of five hundred students, that means only $1.50 is spent annually per child, when the total per pupil annual expenditure in our public schools often exceeds $12,000.[4]

This last statistic is truly a shocker, almost impossible to believe. We know how essential exercise is to good health. We know about the important role it plays in cognition and in reducing stress and anxiety. If these were the only benefits of physical education, they would be more than enough to justify a central place in the curriculum for PE class. In addition, well-taught physical education can improve students' self-control, team cooperation, social skills, and self-confidence. It can teach them to challenge themselves with personal goals, and it affords opportunities to lead and to encourage others.

Teaching physical literacy

Few people know more about what constitutes well-taught physical education than Dr. Frances Cleland. As president of the Society of Health and Physical Educators (SHAPE America), she heads the organization whose standards for K–12 physical education serve as the foundation for PE programs in all fifty states. Dr. Cleland is also coauthor of a highly regarded textbook, *Developmental Physical Education for All Children: Theory Into Practice*, now in its fifth edition.[5]

Born in a little railroad town in northeast Indiana, Fran Cleland knew from the time she was a sophomore in high school that she wanted to teach PE. As a child, when she wasn't swimming or biking, she was jumping on the pogo sticks or walking on the stilts her father made for her. She later developed a passion for modern dance and danced professionally for a time. Dr. Cleland went to Purdue University and taught physical education in several locations around the country before pursuing her doctorate at Indiana University and beginning to teach kinesiology at the university level. She has done this now for almost three decades.

Having worked in the field for so many years, Dr. Cleland has seen a lot of change in physical education. "When I first started teaching," she explains, "not one state had standards for grade-level outcomes in physical education. They may have existed for English or math, but they certainly did not exist for health education or physical education. Our first standards were published in 1995. We then started to base our instruction on children's cognitive, social, and affective development status. Not all kids in the same grade are at the same place developmentally, and we want all children to be engaged in physical education at all times. We want instruction to be differentiated. We also want children to be in control of their own learning, to have choice and input into what they do and how they do it. Physical education is not one size fits all today."[6]

We tend to use "physical education" and "physical activity" interchangeably, but it's important to know the difference between the two. Contrary to what many people think, physical education is about much more than physical activity. While a good PE class always includes physical activity, this is not always true in the reverse. Mere movement doesn't necessarily *teach* anything.

Physical education is about helping students become physically literate and is the foundation of a long-term commitment to fitness.[7] A physically literate individual not only shows proficiency in a variety of movement skills but also recognizes the value of physical activity for health, enjoyment, challenge, self-expression, and/or social interaction.[8] As Dr. Cleland puts it, "Physical literacy is the ability to move with competence and confidence in a wide variety of physical activities in multiple environments that benefit the healthy development of the whole person."[9] A good physical educator deploys a creative range of standards-based, developmentally appropriate ways to involve the student in sequential learning, using a spectrum of teaching styles. Dr. Cleland recommends every physical educator ask, "What am I teaching today? Why am I teaching it? And how do I know my kids have learned?"[10]

So physical education today is not your grandma's gym class! A good PE class is intentionally taught to give students the knowledge and skills to achieve and maintain a healthy level of physical activity and fitness for a lifetime. You could say that it combines movement with minds. Active children who have not had sufficient physical education in school may lack the motivation and know-how to stay fit in their adult years.

Sports are great—but not enough!

Here, perhaps, I should make another important distinction—that is, between PE and sports. I am a huge fan of playing sports. Aside from the fact that all sports can contribute to fitness, they help develop character and teach leadership and teamwork. But most children do not play sports. Therefore, I believe schools need to focus on the fitness basics that all kids need and can do—and that are the foundation for being able to play sports with confidence and competence. The truth of the matter is that school sports tend to be exclusionary based on ability, and there are many barriers to engaging in organized sports, whether school- or community-based. This is especially the case among children from low-income families. Barriers include the cost of equipment and the time and transportation needed to practice and travel to games.[11] In some families, older children might need to spend their time out of school looking after younger siblings or working a job. Moreover, recreational sports like travel soccer have become quite serious, turning off kids who just want to have fun or who are not very good at sports. There are numerous other circumstances, including physical and cognitive disabilities, that do not permit some children to play organized sports.

In sum, sports are wonderful for those who are motivated, have the ability, and are able to engage in them—and who can afford the time and sometimes the money to do so. But it should be incumbent for schools to offer physical education to all children, especially those who don't participate in sports, which is the great majority of students. Furthermore, learning how to stay active outside of sports is a key component of a healthy life; some 70 percent of kids drop out of organized sports by the age of thirteen,[12] and most adults don't play sports regularly again after their school days—and generally not often enough to become fit.

Why schools fall down on the PE job

Schools are in a unique position to provide fitness opportunities to children. Why, then, do so few schools follow the recommended guidelines for physical education or even require recess? Two reasons loom large: misplaced priorities and budget concerns. But what it essentially boils down to, in Dr. Cleland's words, is "administrators' ignorance of the benefits of physical education. We have to develop an academic child, a social child, and a moving child."[13]

Although a 2013 study showed that 84 percent of adults support government policies to add more physical activity time in schools,[14] schools continue to cut PE. This has especially been the case since 2001, when the No Child Left Behind Act (NCLB) was passed. The act sought to improve school accountability by mandating standardized testing nationwide to determine whether children can move up to the next grade or graduate from high school. This became known as "high-stakes" testing because poor results had such a big impact, both on students and on schools. This is not the place to debate the merits of NCLB, but certainly its high-stakes testing meant that schools zeroed in on academics, particularly math, reading, and writing, and made cuts in physical education and the arts. According to the same *Educating the*

Student Body report I cited earlier, "[N]early half of school administrators report cutting significant amounts of time from physical education, art, music, and recess to increase time in reading and mathematics since passage of the No Child Left Behind Act in 2001. Despite the mountain of evidence that physical fitness increases mental acuity and academic performance, these challenges have been cited as the reasons why the percentage of schools offering physical education daily or at least three days each week declined dramatically in US schools between 2000 and 2006."[15]

In 2015, the No Child Left Behind Act was replaced by the Every Student Succeeds Act (ESSA). At the time of its enactment, this was considered a victory for advocates of physical education because it shifted educational goals from mastery of "core subjects" to giving students a "well-rounded education." It also authorized significant funding for health and PE through a block grant program to states. However, Congress only appropriated a quarter of the authorized amount in FY2017, and there is a significant risk, as I write in early 2018, that health and physical education in schools will be greatly underfunded in the next fiscal year. Moreover, while ESSA encourages PE as part of a "well-rounded education," such an education has other components too, such as art and music, and all of them compete for scarce resources. ESSA's block grants replace the only funding that was available specifically for PE from the U.S. Department of Education through the Carol M. White Physical Education Program (known as "PEP" grants). Unfortunately, this program, which provided $24 million for physical education in 2016,[16] its final year, no longer exists.[17] So while ESSA is a step in the right direction, it does not ensure that schoolchildren will get all the physical education they should have.

Alas, despite all we know about the extraordinary benefits of physical education, there are no national requirements for PE in the United States. Instead, each state sets its own, and requirements vary broadly. Here is the good and bad news according to the 2016 *Shape of the Nation*[18] report published by SHAPE America:

- All states but Iowa have adopted standards for PE programs in schools.
- Most states require students to engage in PE in elementary school (thirty-nine states), middle school/junior high (thirty-seven), and high school (thirty-three). Unfortunately, PE in high school is often not required all four years.
- More than half of states require some kind of student assessment.

However, at the same time:

- Only Oregon and the District of Columbia meet the national recommendations for weekly time in PE at both the elementary and middle school levels, when kids should be developing good fitness habits.
- Most states do not set any minimum amount of time for PE at any level.
- Thirty-one states permit other activities to substitute for PE credit, and thirty states allow student exemptions; fifteen states permit school districts to request waivers from the state PE requirements.
- A number of states permit physical education to be completed online. While this may be acceptable in limited circumstances when children are unable to participate in school-based PE, such as for students located in remote geographical areas, students with special needs, or working students, online courses generally fall short in ensuring our children get the physical activity and education they need.

So physical education in the United States is an inconsistent patchwork of requirements, and I think it's safe to say that fitness is far from the norm in our schools and that too few children have the opportunity to become physically literate.

Components of effective physical education

Moreover, where PE is taught, it is not always taught in a way that keeps kids moving and motivated throughout the class period, including those with disabilities and less athletic children. Truly effective physical education should combine quantity of class time with quality of instruction and the same regular assessment of results as academic subjects receive. This requires a curriculum that is based on established standards setting out what students should know and be able to do, as well as one that is designed to keep students moderately to vigorously active for at least half the class time.[19] Assessment protocols should establish whether the student is reaching the benchmark for physical activeness and acquiring the necessary knowledge and skills.[20]

In addition, physical education teachers should have appropriate certification, training (including professional development), and supervision. Studies have shown that certified physical educators are more effective than classroom teachers are in delivering PE lessons and in keeping students moving at a more intense level.[21] This stands to reason given the rigorous certification process and the fact that many physical educators today hold master's degrees. Just as you would probably not consider your child's PE teacher qualified to teach Shakespeare, there is no reason to expect English instructors to know how to teach a great PE class.

Four state-specific PE explorations

One of the greatest challenges facing PE in our schools today is the lack of federal mandates surrounding physical education. There is no federal law requiring minimum standards for physical education in schools.[22] In addition, there are no federal directives to offer physical education programs. This arrangement leaves all implementation up to individual states. Furthermore, policy recommendations at the state level are often very broad, which frequently results in implementation falling to the district level. As a result, there exists a sharp disparity in physical education offerings at the district level within individual states. Without a singular and unified system, students must rely on the discretion of their schools and districts to provide the physical activity and physical education that growing children require for healthy development.

A quick survey of varying state requirements pertaining to physical education is illuminating, especially when compared with current obesity and health trends.

I have chosen four states reflecting a range of PE approaches and obesity prevalence: Mississippi, Oregon, New York, and California. For this comparison, we will look at the relevant obesity and wellness data in the context of the state mandates for physical education, using the following assessments:

- The 2016 *Shape of the Nation* report from SHAPE America.[23]
- Results from the 2015 *Youth Risk Behavior Survey* (YRBS),[24] which is administered by the Centers for Disease Control to monitor priority health risk behaviors among youth in the United States. We will focus specifically on the physical activity findings.
- Findings from the 2016 *State of Obesity* report put together by the Trust for America's Health and the Robert Wood Johnson Foundation using data from the 2016 National Survey of Children's Health.[25]

Here is a quick review of terminology to understand fully the state-by-state findings. First it will be helpful to know the difference between being obese and overweight. Both have to do with the ratio between someone's weight and height, called the body mass index (BMI), and both lead to increased health risks. Overweight individuals have a BMI of between twenty-five and twenty-nine, and obese individuals have a BMI over thirty.

Another important distinction to keep in mind is the difference between physical education and physical activity. As we've discussed, physical education refers to a planned standards-based program with proper instruction to develop student motor skills along with student knowledge about healthy habits and behaviors. Physical activity is simply bodily movement of any type. An activity such as recess may provide physical activity but does not count as physical education. Physical education is of the utmost importance, as it gives students useful information about health and wellness while also providing an opportunity for standards-based physical activity.

It will also be helpful to remember some of the previous trends discussed earlier in the book. For example, children who are inactive are significantly more likely than their fit peers to develop into sedentary adults. In addition, there is a direct correlation between inactivity, obesity, and a number of illnesses.

Mississippi

- Of ten- to seventeen-year-olds, 37 percent are either obese or overweight—the third highest percentage of fifty states.
- The adult obesity rate is 37.3 percent—the second highest percentage in the country.
- The high school obesity rate is 18.9 percent—the highest percentage in the country.
- The current adult diabetes rate is 13.6 percent—the second highest percentage in the country.
- In the 2015 YRBS, 22.9 percent of high school student participants did not participate in at least 60 minutes of physical activity on at least one day during the previous seven days. Of high school respondents, 65.8 percent were not active at least 60 minutes per day on five or more days during the previous seven days. Both of these numbers were the worst of all thirty-seven state participants.
- Mississippi requires 0.5 credits in physical education for high school graduation.

- Middle school students are required to take physical education for 50 minutes per week. There is no minimum time requirement for high school physical education or physical activity.
- Student assessment is required in fifth grade and the high school grade where students receive their necessary 0.5 credits for graduation. There is no particular state-required assessment.

New York

- Of ten- to seventeen-year-olds, 31.8 percent are either obese or overweight—the twentieth highest rate of fifty states.
- The adult obesity rate is 25.5 percent—the forty-fourth highest rate in the country.
- In high school students, 13.1 percent are obese—twentieth in the country.
- The adult diabetes rate is 10.5 percent—twenty-fifth in the country.
- In the 2015 YRBS, 18.8 percent of high school student participants did not participate in at least 60 minutes of physical activity on at least one day during the previous seven days (sixth worst of thirty-seven participants). Of the high school respondents, 58.2 percent were not active for at least 60 minutes per day on five or more days during the previous seven days (seventh worst of thirty-seven state participants).
- New York requires two credits of physical education to graduate high school.
- Physical education in elementary school is mandated for 120 minutes per week. For middle school and high school, physical education is required for at least 90 minutes per week, not less than three times per week in one semester and two times per week in the other semester. There is no required minimum number of minutes for physical activity at any grade level.
- The state does not require a student physical fitness assessment.

Oregon

- Of ten- to seventeen-year-olds, 20.3 percent are either obese or overweight—best out of fifty states.
- The adult obesity rate is 28.7 percent—thirty-first highest rate in the country.
- High school obesity data was not reported.
- The adult diabetes rate is 9.5 percent—thirty-third in the country.
- CDC Youth Risk Behavior Survey data is not available for Oregon.
- Oregon requires one credit in physical education for high school graduation.
- The state requires students to take physical education in grades K–8.
- Elementary students must participate in at least 150 minutes of physical education per week. Middle school students must participate in 225 minutes of physical education per week. There is no minimum amount of time required for physical activity at any grade level.
- The state does not require a physical fitness assessment.
- As mentioned earlier, Oregon is the only state, along with the District of Columbia, that meets the national recommended activity requirements for elementary and middle school students.

California

- Of ten- to seventeen-year-olds, 31.2 percent are either obese or overweight—the twenty-fourth highest obesity rate of fifty states.
- The adult obesity rate is 25 percent—forty-seventh in the country.
- The high school obesity rate is 13.9 percent—seventeenth in the country.

- The current adult diabetes rate is 10.2 percent—twenty-ninth in the country.
- In the 2015 YRBS, 13.1 percent of high school student participants did not participate in at least 60 minutes of physical activity on at least one day during the previous seven days (thirty-first of thirty-seven state participants). Of high school respondents, 51.9 percent were not active at least 60 minutes per day on five or more days during the previous seven days (twenty-eighth out of thirty-seven state participants).
- California requires two years of physical education classes (two credits) to graduate from high school.
- Students in grades one to six must take 200 minutes of physical education every ten days. Students in grades seven through twelve must take 400 minutes of physical education every ten days. There are no specific minute requirements for physical activity.
- Student fitness assessment is required in grades five, seven, and nine, using the FitnessGram.

There is a lot of telling information in the state comparisons above. While a number of factors play into obesity and inactivity numbers, some strong correlations are worth mentioning. Mississippi, for example, is one of the leading states when it comes to high inactivity statistics and elevated obesity numbers for all age groups. Mississippi also has some of the weakest physical education requirements, with a lack of fitness assessment, a shockingly low recommendation for time spent in PE, and a minimal graduation requirement. It is no wonder that a state with such loose physical education mandates produces such high incidences of obesity and inactivity.

Oregon, on the other hand, is the only state, along with the District of Columbia, that meets national recommendations for physical activity in grades K–8. The result? Their students are among the fittest in the country! New York falls somewhere between Mississippi and Oregon, with moderate PE requirements and neutral outcomes. Finally,

California has extensive physical education requirements, including detailed minute recommendations, clear graduation requirements, and mandated fitness testing. When looking at Youth Risk Behavior Survey data, it is evident that California students are some of the best performing students with regard to weekly physical activity. Compared to Mississippi, California requires four times as much physical education to graduate, along with four times the required physical education minutes for middle school students. It should be no surprise that California outperforms Mississippi across the board in all measures of obesity and physical activity.

In sum, fitness and physical literacy are critically important aspects of a child's wellness. Eventually, children need to own their health, which is what a good physical education program teaches them to do. In the meantime, we owe it to our children to provide quality physical education and fitness opportunities in school.

Crucial takeaways

- In the words of President Kennedy, "The physical fitness of our citizens is a vital prerequisite to America's realization of its full potential as a nation, and to the opportunity of each individual citizen to make full and fruitful use of his capacities."
- Not one state follows the recommendations from the Centers for Disease Control for time spent in PE at all grade levels.
- Competing priorities and budget limitations have crowded out physical education in schools. However, PE is far too important to neglect for its academic, as well as its physical and mental, benefits.
- Our children need standards-based physical education that teaches them physical literacy so that they value and know how to attain a fit lifestyle into adulthood.
- Well-taught physical education can improve students' self-control, team cooperation, social skills, and self-confidence. It

can teach them to challenge themselves with personal goals, and it affords opportunities to lead and to encourage others.

- Schools need to extend their focus from sports to the fitness basics all children need.

5

LET'S GET PHYSICAL: TWO EDUCATORS SHARE THEIR PERSPECTIVES

Two outstanding physical educators

It's easy to see why the California Association for Health, Physical Education, Recreation and Dance honored both Christine Berni-Ramos and John Kruse as Physical Education Teacher of the Year. Both of them are passionate about what they do and genuinely concerned about the students they teach. In addition, Christine and John both went through the rigorous process to become national board-certified teachers and hold master's degrees in educational administration and special education, respectively.

Christine grew up in East Los Angeles, where she had an exceptional PE teacher in middle school who recognized her skill in sports and her potential as a leader. "He helped me gain confidence and believe in myself, which gave me the courage to join team sports and compete in middle and high school,"[1] she recalls. Sports also kept her out of trouble in a community with its share of gangs and drugs, so Christine knows from personal experience how inspirational the right teacher/ mentor can be. She is committed to being the same kind of motivator and providing support to her own students. "Teachers of physical education, coaches, and mentors can make or break the experience for students," Christine says. "Great leaders create positive experiences and influence all learners."[2] Additionally, she became a district teacher leader and mentor to support classroom teachers required to teach PE as well as physical educators new to the field. For twenty-three years, ever since she got her degree from Cal State Long Beach, Christine has taught physical education to middle and high schoolers at the Elizabeth Learning Center in Cudahy, California (part of Los Angeles County, with one of the highest population densities of any incorporated city in the country). This kind of longevity at one school is rare for teachers of any subject and gives Christine an unusually long-term perspective on physical education and how it has changed over the years.

John also grew up in Southern California, playing baseball, basketball, and soccer, but didn't really find his athletic niche until he took up cycling while earning a Boy Scout merit badge in the sport. "The Boy Scout program had a huge influence on me," John says. "Interestingly, scouting has three aims that are very much in line with the field of physical education. These include personal fitness, character development, and leadership. The skill set I learned on the trail to Eagle Scout really paid dividends as a teacher."[3]

Despite having exercise-induced asthma, John was a serious cycler all the way through college at Cal State Northridge and strengthened his lungs to the point where he no longer needed to use an inhaler. As a result, John came to appreciate firsthand the power of exercise to improve health. On track to become a special education science teacher, a discussion with a group of physical educators at the school where he was teaching made him decide to change course. He realized he had a great deal in common with them, as physical education is a science-based discipline, and he wanted to share with kids all he had learned about the healthful benefits of fitness. He taught PE for over ten years and is now K–12 physical education advisor for a major public school system in California. Among his other responsibilities, he supports PE teachers district-wide by giving them curriculum advice and steering them to professional development opportunities that enhance standards-based instruction. He also ensures that California's physical education requirements are met in each school. John has contributed two chapters to a textbook for physical educators: *Lesson Planning for Middle School Physical Education: Meeting the National Standards & Grade-Level Outcomes.*[4]

Physical education as preventive medicine

John and Christine both stress the difference between physical activity and physical education. "Having an exercise science background, I was really into the FitnessGram and fitness scores," John said. "I almost viewed myself as a personal trainer for the kids. I was always looking for those fitness results and wanted to see improvement. Then I realized that learning should be my primary instructional goal; my kids needed to learn how to be physically literate."[5]

Christine remarks, "Children need to be prepared for fitness testing, but they need to apply what they've learned into adulthood. We want to make them knowledgeable exercisers and skillful movers who value physical activity and a healthy lifestyle when they are older."[6]

"I see physical education as preventive medicine," John says. "Athletics are important, but the reality is that being an elite-level athlete doesn't necessarily guarantee that you're going to be a healthy person for the rest of your life. Look at all the overweight and obese baseball coaches we have. They're all former athletes, but they clearly didn't have the skill set to remain physically active and healthy for the rest of their lives. This is what we teach in physical education. So many conditions that are treated with drugs these days, like high cholesterol and hypertension, could be addressed with exercise first."[7]

John recognizes that a number of health professionals still see physical education primarily as a time for physical activity. "I get that," he says, "because sometimes the students are living in neighborhoods where parents don't feel safe with their being outdoors, and so physical education at the school site could be the only place that's safe for them to be active. I have that fear with my own kids when I see cars flying down our street. But I want to hammer home that physical education promotes lifelong good health and is about more than just giving kids exercise. That's important, but if we don't teach kids for the long term, it's going to cost us taxpayers a ton. To a significant extent, one can be one's own doctor basically by being a physically educated person."[8]

Changing trends

John notes that the trend away from a sports-based model of PE to a health-related fitness model has been going on for the past twenty years. He believes that this is "a trend that will continue owing to the brain-based research that we're seeing. The link between exercise and the brain will continue to influence this. When I go to conferences these days, there's more and more awareness of the effects of brain-derived neurotropic factor (BDNF) and all the ways exercise helps the brain power up. I think it's probably going to take some time for school systems and parents to recognize this, but it's beginning to happen."[9]

When Christine began teaching twenty-three years ago, she recollects there was no PE curriculum at the school. "Everybody just kind of taught whatever they felt like they needed to do, or what they liked best, what the teacher liked, which didn't always meet the learning needs of the kids. The equipment was just basic, traditional equipment like basketballs [and] volleyballs—and nothing outside of the box or different to help kids develop their skills. I saw there wasn't enough for the kids and there was just little to no learning going on, so that's when I decided to grow myself first by getting national board certified in 2004."[10]

Today, Christine approaches every class with physical education standards in mind and creates assessment tools for student learning outcomes according to their grade levels. She says it's important to create early positive experiences that keep kids wanting more PE and to give them a say in what "fun" is. Her goal is to engage all students in a class and to encourage them to focus on doing their "personal best" rather than on whether they win or lose.

Social and emotional learning in physical education

Christine notes that PE teaches more than fitness or even good health habits: "Several studies have researched the link between PE and cooperative learning. [Students] learn the importance of leadership, team building, collaboration, self-management, respecting differences, and encouragement through group physical activities. There is a whole side of PE that is about social and emotional well-being."[11]

John Kruse echoes Christine on this point. "There's a huge emphasis on social and emotional learning in our field, and teamwork, and being able to be a follower and a leader, and decision-making processes. All of this is part of our content as well. When you think about it, that's probably equally as important as all the fitness and physical activity, because my understanding is that the Fortune 500 companies' number one complaint is that their employees don't know how to work and play well with each other. So that's a huge part of our job, giving students the skill set to be able to work with each other, which will carry into their work world one day."[12]

Obesity epidemic starts at an early age

Both John and Christine are concerned about the high obesity rate among students. Children often enter middle school with significant weight problems already, and overall Christine estimates that 60 to 70 percent of the middle and high school students at Elizabeth Learning Center are overweight. (Across the LAUSD as a whole, in the 2016–2017 school year, approximately half the children mandated to take the FitnessGram test in grades 5, 7, and 9 were not in the Healthy Fitness Zone for body composition.)[13] John puts a large part of the blame on "portion distortion" and on the fact that "we've basically engineered the gross motor movements out of our society through escalators, cars, elevators, and so on. Now we're working on the fine motor movements too—we don't even have to turn the dial anymore. Then there's too much screen time. I'm not one of the people who say smartphones are all bad. I think they're a useful tool, but we need to get kids to put them away more than they do. All of these factors have come together to create the obesity epidemic."[14]

Opportunities for better parent communication

While schools are doing a better job of providing nutritious meals to students and of teaching kids about the importance of various food groups and how they interact with the body, Christine identifies a need for more parent education and involvement. Elizabeth Learning Center does have a family center on campus where parents can find out about the benefits of healthful eating and exercise, but she notes, "It's always the same parents of the same kids who come; we need to get to the other parents. It's difficult for many parents to get there, I know, but I think that would really help."[15]

Christine recommends homework assignments where parents and children work together to learn about the impact poor nutrition can have as well as the benefits of fitness. She would like to see school-wide fitness-oriented events like a "fun run," where staff, teachers, parents, and kids can all enjoy being together.

Christine is a fan of the FitnessGram because "it is a research-based test in which they've made many changes throughout the years for the better."[16] But she believes schools should seize the opportunity when FitnessGram results are sent home, as required by the state, to give parents more detailed information about the health risks associated with poor fitness and obesity. She believes that all students should be provided with the opportunity to take the FitnessGram, not only those in the grades mandated to take it, so that they can receive feedback, practice, and improve.

Dr. Kimberly Uyeda, the former LAUSD director of student medical services, also views the FitnessGram as a chance to engage in discussion with parents and sees a need to "open up the communication channels around what the schools are doing about physical education and testing. It seems like a great opportunity for us to send a message and to elevate some of what research shows about physically active people doing better on tests and having better graduation rates. We need to do a better job of acknowledging the role that physical education and health education have in overall student achievement and wellness."[17]

Other ways to promote fitness and health

Christine and John lament the prevalence of fast-food stores and restaurants near schools. These are a big draw to older students when they leave campus. Several studies[18] have shown that students at schools within a half mile of fast-food restaurants and convenience stores are more likely to be overweight or obese than students attending school farther away. They are also less likely to eat fruits and vegetables and more inclined to drink soda.

Smaller class sizes, Christine says, would help her provide better physical education. Over the years, she has had classes as big as seventy students, which means more discipline problems, inadequate safety, and fewer minutes of activity as students line up to use scarce equipment. Her ideal class size would be thirty, to be more consistent with other subject areas, but she'd settle for a cap of forty students, which would still be a reasonably manageable class size.

Some schools are experimenting with more kinesthetic classrooms, an approach that John Kruse finds appealing. Classes could have more three- to five-minute physical activity breaks, for instance, whether standing up at one's desk or doing movements with some degree of complexity to challenge the brain. "I shared some of those brain-based activities with an English teacher, and he thought they were so great [that] he bought them for the entire department," John recollects.[19]

The power of a great teacher

As a master physical educator, Christine encourages critical thinking in her students about what they eat and the consequences of choosing one food over another at a meal so they know, for instance, how long they might need to exercise in order to work off the calories from a particular treat. She brainstorms with them on how to get their recommended minutes of physical activity, and she works hard to motivate students. She recalls one ninth grade girl who was struggling to reach the Healthy Fitness Zone in aerobic activity, and who was "always so sad and frustrated, and wanted to improve. She saw the importance, and I really wanted to help her. She would come into our fitness center, and I would help her create a realistic plan with incremental goals to improve over time. By the tenth grade, she passed the aerobic capacity section of the test and lowered her BMI. She was so proud and ended up joining the cross-country team as a result. She became a runner, which was not something she thought she could ever do."[20]

This young woman succeeded not only because of her own determination but also because she had a physical education teacher who encouraged her along the way. In Christine's words, "I think the kids need to know that you really care about them. If you give them that feeling that you really care and you're genuine about what you tell them, they take it to heart and apply it. What I really would like them to know about obesity is that it's dangerous to their health, and it saddens me to see some kids that are overweight now and to think about the [lives that] they are likely to lead in the future as far as being on medication or [having] prediabetes. I want them to understand that it's no joke; it's to be taken very seriously."[21]

Crucial takeaways

- Physical education is preventive medicine.
- Opportunities exist to expand parental involvement and education concerning PE and health.
- Physical education not only teaches lessons about lifelong fitness and health, but also has a significant social and emotional component. It prepares students for the workforce by teaching cooperation and teamwork—along with many other social skills.

- Class size needs to be controlled for the optimum learning in physical education, and schools can look for ways to create more kinesthetic classrooms.
- Committed physical education teachers like John Kruse and Christine Berni-Ramos can make a huge difference in children's health and fitness.

6

BREAK A SWEAT, CHANGE YOUR LIFE: THE STORY OF UCLA HEALTH SOUND BODY SOUND MIND

In the last few chapters, I have discussed the dangers of inactivity as well as the benefits of exercise and reported generally on the state of physical education on our schools today. Now I want to tell you about UCLA Health Sound Body Sound Mind, the program I mentioned in the introduction, which my wife, Cindy, and I started in 1998 as a response to the growing obesity epidemic in Los Angeles, where we live. I tell this story for two reasons: partly as a way to commemorate our twentieth year in operation (2018) and partly as an example of what private initiatives can accomplish. I hope that others might learn from our experience and replicate our program in other cities.

The beginning: a unique opportunity

At the beginning of the book, I described the life lessons physical fitness taught me as a young man. Fast-forward now from my twenties in law school to my middle years in Los Angeles. By 1997, my wonderful wife and I were blessed with four great kids, and I had gotten some significant material success under my belt in the investment business. It was time to give back. So when a neighbor asked Cindy and me to donate some fitness equipment to our local high school in Pacific Palisades, we happily agreed. We both knew what fitness had done for us, and this seemed like a great way to encourage the kids in our area to get more exercise.

The equipment was installed in our hometown at Pacific Palisades High School in December 1998, and although we didn't know it then, this turned out to be the first of over 127 (as of this writing in 2018) fitness centers we set up in Los Angeles area schools. The second was for the school in our Catholic parish, St. Monica's. Word spread quickly, and other neighboring schools in need of PE equipment approached us as well. We helped them too.

As our mini-program grew, we began to read more about the dangerous obesity epidemic in Los Angeles, where 42 percent of children are overweight[1] and 22 percent of children in grades five, seven, and nine are obese.[2] We heard how the problem was particularly acute in low-income and minority communities where there is limited access to safe parks and playgrounds, an abundance of fast-food restaurants, and limited budgets for more expensive, healthy food.[3] Schools were often the only venue where kids could exercise, yet, as I discussed earlier, PE budgets were notoriously limited and most resources went to support academic or athletic programs, with next to nothing left over to get the average student moving. While recognizing that the obesity problem cannot be solved with exercise alone, we felt it was an area in which we could make a real difference and benefit all children, whether overweight or not. We seem to have stumbled upon something very important we could do—a truly unique opportunity.

At first, we had a loose, easygoing kind of approach. We set up fitness centers with twenty to twenty-two pieces of state-of-the-art equipment, had a ribbon-cutting ceremony, and presented award certificates at the end of the school year. However, we really did not do much else. Soon, as we began to understand the overall demographic and landscape, Cindy and I realized that if we wanted to be really effective in fighting the growing obesity epidemic, we needed an ongoing relationship with the schools and an organized game plan to take us into the future. We also knew we'd need some financial help from others to expand the program and meet the huge demand for fitness resources in the wake of school budget cutbacks. Our fitness equipment cost fifty thousand dollars per school to install, a hefty up-front sum and yet quite cost-effective when you consider the thousands of students who utilize our equipment over many years.

So we created a charitable foundation, which we named Sound Body Sound Mind because we were committed to the idea that the synergy between the two creates an optimally healthy and productive person. We then set about finding some outside funding to supplement our own contributions so we could reach more schools and work on building a more sophisticated program.

Luck was certainly on our side! My wife's close friend and trainer, Donna Fol, had seen something about the availability of federal "PEP" (Physical Education Program) grants. We asked Alexander Kowell, a recent Harvard graduate we'd hired to help us out while he looked for a job in his intended career, to take a crack at applying. Almost beyond belief, we were successful. Our upstart nonprofit received $1.5 million from the United States government to expand its program! It was a huge shot in the arm for us.

Laying the groundwork: our first executive director

We got word of the grant just a week before Alex was set to move on, and Emily Ernsdorf Fritz became our first official executive director in 2004. She did a great job during our initial expansion period, managing the PEP grant, growing the program, and laying the groundwork for a broader fundraising effort, which included a promotional video featuring Paula Abdul, Al Michaels, and Tommy Lasorda. She also began partnerships with our first special needs schools. Kids with special needs are markedly less active than other youth, and often do not fully participate in recess, playground games, or organized sports. Yet they need to acquire the physical, mental, and social benefits of physical activity just as much as other kids do, if not more so. Therefore, we were very excited to be able to reach kids with intellectual or physical disabilities. Emily recently told me, "I will never forget the faces of the parents of special needs students at our ribbon-cutting ceremonies. The children in these schools had varying disabilities and rarely had an opportunity to participate in organized sports or physical education. The parents were overjoyed that their kids were having so much fun while getting some exercise."[4]

Our early hiring system: mentoring young staff

Emily was the first of a number of recent college graduates who came to us over the next several years, many from UCLA, as we began to implement a special hiring policy that worked beautifully for all involved at the time. Our system then was to hire recent graduates, often with backgrounds in kinesiology, mentor them for two to six years on the job, and then push them out of the nest to the next stop on their career paths. In this way, our young staff got some significant work experience under their belts, along with more responsibility than they would generally have had elsewhere so early in their professional lives. They were able to build their confidence and qualifications while they thought about their future career directions. We always promoted our executive directors from within, so they learned some leadership as well. Sound Body Sound Mind, in turn, benefitted from the energy, creativity, and can-do spirit of young graduates while keeping its salary costs at a more moderate level than it would have been able to do with more seasoned hires. It was always hard to say goodbye to our staff as they moved on, but I am overjoyed at how they flourished and am pleased that our organization could provide valuable early opportunity and training for them. We have continued to stay in touch with many of them as they have moved on to successful careers and raising their own families.

Developing the right equipment for all

Scott MacKenzie, a recent graduate of my alma mater, Williams College, moved up into Emily's position in the summer of 2007, at which time we were in forty schools. Scott introduced nutritional literature into the program and identified a less expensive fitness provider, Matrix Fitness, which allowed us to offer additional equipment at the same cost. Some of our older equipment was wearing out, and Scott oversaw our repair and replace efforts where needed. Rick Baza was an independent equipment consultant to us at the time and an enormous support in working through equipment issues. He helped us choose the equipment we gave schools very carefully so that there was a good mix of cardiovascular equipment such as commercial grade spin bikes, rowers, and ellipticals.

We continued to develop our relationship with schools for kids with special needs and made a commitment to provide customized equipment that works for the populations of each of our schools, many of which have nonambulatory students as well as students facing cognitive challenges. Today I am pleased to say that our team has put significant time and effort into supporting our special needs schools, with programs in eleven schools in Los Angeles.

Our first big gala: funding our expansion into middle schools

By 2008, the PEP funds had been largely exhausted and we needed to raise more money. So in April of that year, we had our first big gala, which marked our tenth anniversary and the beginning of what I call the modern era at Sound Body Sound Mind. We had two co-executive directors at that time, Adrianna Johnson ("AJ") and Lindsay Payne, and together they mounted an extremely successful event. Among our five hundred guests at the Beverly Wilshire Hotel were thirty-five former Olympians, including distance runner and World War II hero Louis Zamperini. We raised some three million dollars that evening, and our success marked a new phase for Sound Body Sound Mind. It also enabled us to expand into middle schools, which was very important to our mission. AJ considers this her greatest accomplishment while she was at Sound Body Sound Mind, as "engaging students in fitness at a younger age makes them more likely to maintain physical fitness when they become adults."[5]

Evaluating our early years

By now, the basics of our program were well established. We'd learned a lot by trial and error, and we'd been in business long enough to begin to notice some issues in the schools. In order to understand fully what was going on and to see how we could best support our schools, we set about visiting those where we had installed a fitness center. These visits were decidedly eye-opening, and we learned a great deal from them. It was clear that not all schools were maintaining our equipment in good condition. We also struggled at some schools with ensuring a high utilization rate of our fitness centers; it was not always easy to keep teachers and students engaged after the initial excitement of having a state-of-the-art facility wore off. Moreover, there were always problems with turnover of administrators and teachers, so there was not enough accountability or consistency in how the equipment was used.

In response to these concerns, we took several steps. We invited schools with strong fitness programs, but whose budgets would not cover repair costs, to apply for equipment maintenance grants. We implemented a more robust contract with schools so that it was clear what our mutual responsibilities were. In addition, we set about developing a curriculum and teacher training program that would ensure our equipment was used to the greatest effect.

Developing our curriculum

Keith Legro and Nathan Nambiar, two UCLA graduates who joined our staff in 2008 and 2009, respectively, spearheaded the curriculum design. They did a terrific job, and both of them eventually moved into the executive director position. Working with Jim Liston, founder of the Competitive Athlete Training Zone (CATZ), a leading provider of youth sports performance training, they wrote a curriculum that would not only keep kids moving in PE class but also one that would motivate them to lead healthier lifestyles in the years ahead. We also had a good deal of help from Lee Hancock, PhD, a professor in the physical education department at California State University Dominguez Hills. Devising the station-based activities that would give kids a good physical workout without turning off the less energetic ones took some thinking. And since we had begun to install fitness centers in middle schools, we needed to develop a curriculum and equipment mix for these younger students for whom weight equipment wasn't appropriate. The biggest challenge, however, was putting together the social-emotional side of the curriculum. Jim Liston's advice was invaluable. Jim had a real passion for working with kids and a great deal of insight into what makes them tick. He knew the less physically fit kids needed to feel emotionally safe in our program, sure in the knowledge that they would not be made fun of or humiliated and that their efforts would be appreciated. He also recognized that it would be important to have a community-building social aspect of the curriculum to show kids that fitness can be fun. If they didn't enjoy fitness, they wouldn't stick with it.

With the help of Jim and his colleagues at CATZ, we developed a unique curriculum with several specific goals in mind:

- To keep students moving and heart rates elevated, as well as to improve endurance, strength, flexibility, balance, hand-eye coordination, dexterity, and locomotion.
- To teach students fundamental fitness facts so they will have a strong knowledge base to prepare them for active and healthy lifestyles.
- To give students some choice in the tasks they perform so they have more "ownership" of their work. In this way, they are more apt to try activities outside their comfort zones and are less likely to become discouraged.
- To foster a positive, supportive environment for students that enhances self-confidence and motivates them to make healthy lifestyle choices.

- To help teachers manage large classes with options for concurrent exercise on a variety of equipment.
- To develop intrinsic motivation to be physically fit so that students remain active long term. Accordingly, activities in our curriculum are designed to be fun and social.

Our curriculum contains thirty-six flexible lessons designed to create a learning environment that encourages participation by applying several key principles in our teaching:

- Students are greeted by name so they feel it is important they are there.
- Nicknames are not permitted, as you never know how a student feels about his or her nickname.
- Mistakes are good. They are part of practicing and lead to improvement. Only by making mistakes can students step out of their comfort zones and learn.
- Exercise is never used as a punishment. How many times have we seen students disciplined by being told to "Run another lap" or "Give me ten push-ups"? This only encourages students to dislike exercise rather than embrace it.
- Students do not pick teams. The last to be picked will feel discouraged and unmotivated.
- End each class with a "big finish," a group activity to establish a sense of community and sociability and cause students to look forward to the next class.
- Praise should be specific, addressing both the student's performance and practice rather than simply saying "Good job!"
- When introducing a skill, coaches instruct in a process called "tell-show-do." They tell students what the new skill is, show them how to do it, and then have the students attempt it.

Testing the Sound Body Sound Mind Curriculum

By 2010, we had finished writing the curriculum and it was now time to test it. Our trial run occurred at Grant High School in the Valley Glen section of Los Angeles, where Keith and Nathan led an after-school program for six months. "It was an incredible experience to watch kids develop physically and emotionally during this time," Keith told me recently. "We used to give out different colored T-shirts according to how long the kids had participated in the program, and it became very cool to move up the T-shirt ladder, as it were. The veterans helped the new members and learned some leadership. Even the shyest kids came out of their shells to help others master the fitness activities. By the end of the six months, the kids were so proud of their improvement. We had a blast!"[6]

With the implementation of our Sound Body Sound Mind Curriculum, we expanded the range of equipment schools receive. Now, in addition to stationary cardiovascular equipment, schools receive mobile accessories that keep large classes moving more effectively, give a workout to more parts of the body, and make fitness more accessible for students with special needs. This equipment includes SandBell weights for strength training, agility ladders, jump ropes, balls, exercise mats, and cones.

Selecting participating schools

It was an inspiration for our team to work alongside teachers who cared so much about keeping kids healthy and fit and poured themselves into learning the curriculum and how best to deploy the equipment. Nevertheless, there were always some teachers who didn't want to learn a new way of doing things and administrators who resisted change. It was sometimes difficult to know which teachers were excited about our program and which just wanted credit for bringing in some shiny new equipment and would then lose interest. We had to be quite selective in deciding where to invest; not every school was ready for us.

We began to realize the need for a better application and review process, as well as an agreement that required more from the schools so that they truly valued our program and would use our equipment to optimal effect. Today our selection process is multifaceted and allows us to get a full understanding of the physical education environment on each campus. It has three components: a written application, an in-person interview in our offices, and, for each finalist, a site visit to see the facilities and to observe PE classes firsthand. We also have an eye out for a special champion for our program at each of our schools, a key staff member who is truly engaged in the process and willing to be our grant coordinator. Other advocates, such as administrators, are crucial as well. We have been enormously fortunate to work with many exceptional Sound Body Sound Mind champions in our schools over the years, people who are passionate about physical education and about their students and who are essential to our success.

A fresh look at our school contracts

In addition to improving our application process, we also took a fresh look at our contracts with schools. We had made changes in them from time to time based on our experience, and by 2011, they had evolved so that schools were responsible for completing appropriate room renovations before any equipment was installed and for assigning a specific staff member we could work with at the school on any issues that came up. We continue to refine our contract, and today we require all physical educators at newly selected schools to attend a training session on the curriculum. While we recognize that schools have a number of items they must cover in their physical education syllabi and cannot focus exclusively on our curriculum, our equipment and facilities are in use year-round. Last, our contract requires that schools collect data on how well students do on the state-mandated FitnessGram test before and after using our curriculum.

Chad Fenwick was an invaluable colleague who provided crucial assistance to us in drafting the contract and in understanding how the LAUSD worked. A longtime physical education teacher as well as the past president of the California Association for Health, Physical Education, Recreation and Dance (CAHPERD), Chad was a great resource for Sound Body Sound Mind. He knew the dynamics of each school, gave us wonderful guidance in our selection process, and introduced us to teachers who would become champions for our program. He also helped us better appreciate the challenges PE teachers face, such as unmotivated students, large class sizes, inadequate space, and limited class time.

Measuring our effectiveness

By 2013, Nathan Nambiar had stepped into Keith's shoes as executive director. Sound Body Sound Mind was in eighty schools, and we had worked out many of the kinks in our program. Now we needed to find ways to measure its effectiveness more accurately. We knew very well, in an anecdotal way, that kids in our program were reaching a new level of fitness and were more mindful of healthy choices they could make. But we wanted to quantify our success in a comprehensive and academically rigorous way to prove to the school community as well as to donors that Sound Body Sound Mind really produced results and lived up to its motto: "Break a sweat, change your life."

So in 2013, Sound Body Sound Mind partnered with UCLA Professor and Associate Dean Dr. Anastasia Loukaitou-Sideris and the Robert F. Kennedy Community Schools in Los Angeles to evaluate the effectiveness of our program. We were delighted, but not at all surprised, that the study revealed the students participating in the evaluation achieved a dramatic increase in their performance on the FitnessGram test. After completing the Sound Body Sound Mind program, 40 percent more students in the RFK Community Schools achieved passing rates, exceeding the local and statewide average passing rates for their grades. Further, 84 percent of the students affirmed they were more knowledgeable about physical activity and exercise, while teachers said they expected the curriculum would have a long-term impact on students, prompting them to be more active physically in the future. We were extremely pleased to see such significant results, which Dr. Loukaitou-Sideris published in the *Journal of Education and Training Studie*s.[7]

We were enormously excited about this study and eager to share it with our loyal donors and community partners. So in October 2013 we had a "friend-raiser" party at our home to announce the results and thank everyone for their support. Several well-known athletes came, including Wyomia Tyus, the first Olympian to win consecutive gold medals in the 100-meter dash; Dr. Mark Crear, a two-time Olympic medalist in the 110-meter high hurdles; and John Naber, who had earned four gold medals in swimming, each in record time, at the 1976 Olympics. John had been a great supporter of Sound Body Sound Mind since its early days; indeed, it was he who had spread the word about our program among the many star athletes who came to our 2008 gala.

The UCLA report we celebrated at the "friend-raiser" was third party, academic confirmation of our effectiveness, but we continue to measure student achievement internally. This includes monitoring the students' perceptions and attitudes toward physical education as well as the progress they are making in personal fitness. Physical education teachers administer a behavioral survey before and after the implementation of our curriculum, and generally we see students report measurable improvements in healthy behaviors and actions, body image, and enjoyment of fitness. In addition, our students usually achieve a 25 percent increase in FitnessGram passing rates. Of course we want students to improve their overall health through physical fitness while they are in school, but we have a much greater longer-term goal: we want them to understand the importance of maintaining fitness for the rest of their lives.

Partnership with UCLA Health System

By the end of 2014, we were in ninety Los Angeles schools, impacting just over one hundred thousand students a year in grades six through twelve. We were a mature organization, with a staff of four and a dedicated board. It was always a challenge to raise the funds we needed, but we were on a great path and it was time to look to the future. I was sixty-three, and while I was in excellent health—thanks in large part, I'm convinced, to my commitment to daily exercise—I wanted to ensure that Sound Body Sound Mind survived well into the future.

One of our board members at the time was Dr. David Feinberg, then president and chief executive officer of the UCLA Health System which serves some 2.5 million[8] patients a year with cutting-edge medical care. I knew something about UCLA Health because I was a member of the advisory board of its flagship hospital, the Ronald Reagan UCLA Medical Center. An idea began to percolate in my mind: what a lot of punch we could pack if Sound Body Sound Mind and UCLA Health could merge! It seemed like a natural fit: UCLA Health had incredible expertise in health and marketing, a vast and stable infrastructure, and a strong interest in expanding their community engagement. Sound Body Sound Mind had an innovative fitness program that had set hundreds of thousands of Angeleno youth on a path to better health in a way that was scalable, sustainable, and cost-effective. In addition, most of our staff over the years had been UCLA graduates and I was now teaching there. I felt that if we joined forces, both of our organizations could amplify their impact in the Los Angeles community. Sound Body Sound Mind, with its proven track record of success among one of our city's most vulnerable populations, would be a public health ally to UCLA Health; and UCLA Health, with its tremendous community reach and expertise, could help us with public relations, marketing, and fund-raising. And importantly, our alliance would solve my concerns about putting Sound Body Sound Mind on a solid long-term footing after I was no longer as active.

Our executive director, Nathan Nambiar, crafted an excellent proposal, and we sat down with David Feinberg to explore the possibility of a merger. The happy result was that in March 2015, our two organizations joined forces to become UCLA Health Sound Body Sound Mind.

Growing media exposure

Nathan's successor, Patrick McCredie, took us to the next level as we learned to work together. He made sure all aspects of our two organizations, from payroll to press relations, meshed together, no small task. He also organized a "backyard gala" at our home in October 2015 to announce the merger. This was a wonderful evening during which we welcomed Olympic gold medal decathlete Rafer Johnson, former pro-basketball player Tyus Edney, and UCLA Bruins defensive lineman turned actor, Donovan Carter. Ann Meyers Drysdale, one of the greatest stars in the history of basketball and, according to *Time* magazine, one of the top ten greatest women sports pioneers of all time,[9] also honored us by attending.

UCLA Health Sound Body Sound Mind was now in one hundred schools in the Los Angeles Unified School District and getting some real traction in terms of media exposure. In 2015, *U.S. News and World Report* ran an article by Dr. Feinberg on childhood obesity,[10] which zeroed in on our work, and our staff wrote an article on intrinsic motivation in physical education for the *Journal of Physical Education, Recreation and Dance.*[11] Kevin de León, president pro tempore of the California State Senate, spoke at the ribbon cutting at Joseph Le Conte Middle School in 2016, and our local ABC and CBS affiliates both sent reporters to cover the ceremony. We have also been covered by other local stations including Telemundo and Univision. It sure felt as if we had arrived.

Nearing two decades: evaluating and expanding our impact

When Patrick left later that year, Matthew Flesock stepped into his shoes to guide the organization as it approached its twentieth anniversary. Before he became executive director, Matt had already made a substantial contribution to our work by designing and implementing an intensive audit of the first eighty-nine schools in our program. We learned a great deal by making site visits to each school to inspect the facilities and to sit down with their physical educators to find out what was working well for them and what was not. That was when we realized we needed to offer more training for physical education teachers, especially teachers who were new to our schools and had missed the initial training. Moreover, we increased the amount we allocated for maintenance funding from twenty-five to fifty thousand dollars annually so that schools could keep our equipment in good working order. It certainly helped that Matt identified a new, less expensive vendor to do the repairs.

More recently, Matt and his colleague Amanda Gittleman have been instrumental in assembling a stellar academic advisory council for UCLA Health Sound Body Sound Mind, which will provide us with greater insight into the ways in which we can continue to improve our program. Matt, with the help of UCLA Health, has also put together a professional full media package with video downloads[12] illustrating the impact of our work and has established a relationship with the Los Angeles Lakers, which will bring more attention to our program. He is also in charge of our twentieth anniversary gala, which will take place in October 2018 at UCLA's Luskin Conference Center—a wonderful celebration of the community partnerships that have made our work possible.

Twentieth anniversary reflections

As I complete this book in early 2018, Cindy and I could not be more proud—or more amazed—at all UCLA Health Sound Body Sound Mind has accomplished, especially in our own backyard. Over the years, we have helped 750,000 young Angelenos move toward longer and healthier lives through fitness. With 127 fitness centers currently serving over 160,000 students in grades six through twelve every year in Los Angeles, we, together with our generous donors, have contributed more than five million dollars to enhance physical education programs and trained over four hundred educators on our curriculum. We focus primarily on schools in low-income communities and neighborhoods; and across all our schools, over 75 percent of students qualify for free or reduced price lunches. In these areas, our UCLA Health Sound Body Sound Mind kids have few fitness resources outside of school.

We have been especially pleased to hear from physical educators about the impact of our work. Christine Berni-Ramos comments as follows: "The impact of the fitness center has been remarkable. It is evident that it played a key role in the increase of my students' FitnessGram test scores, and it has given them more motivation and self-confidence. Throughout the years, I have observed many of our families and staff—as well as our students—use the fitness center, building their commitment to a healthy, active lifestyle. The fitness center has been an exciting addition for our school and community, and the possibilities have been endless. We have had many success stories, including one student who lost fifty pounds in the year after he started using the center and ended up on our school soccer team."[13]

John Kruse remarks on another aspect of our fitness center's importance: "I saw students who would be more reserved in a team sport scenario who would show another side of themselves in the fitness center. They would really get into the whole strength training aspect or the circuit training part. And I remember one student who was shy about my measuring her height and weight to calculate her BMI, but she was super enthusiastic about the fitness center, always talking about it."[14]

Kenneth Bernas, head of physical education at James Madison Middle School in Los Angeles, reports the following: "I had a student who lost twenty pounds after having the fitness unit in seventh grade and continuing to work out through his eighth grade year. Another PE teacher told me about a student who was struggling with weight and having trouble completing the mile run in less than fifteen minutes. After going through our program, she lost over forty pounds and got her mile time under ten minutes; and when she went on to high school, she made the basketball team."[15]

In light of success stories like these, we were eager to spread our message to other cities. Thanks to the generosity of the Anschutz Foundation, in 2009 we introduced our program to four schools in Denver, Colorado. Led by Denver Public Schools, the program grew to eight schools in the mile-high city. A couple of years later, we trained educators from all 211 schools in the Dallas Independent School District on the Sound Body Sound Mind Curriculum. In total, we are bringing fitness resources to over 170,000 students in 141 schools nationwide on an annual basis. We are excited about our momentum and optimistic about what the future holds in store for our program. We project we will be in 150 schools at the end of the 2018–2019 school year.

I attribute our success to three factors. First, our idea was a simple and eminently practical one: a gift of the right equipment, along with a carefully crafted curriculum and teacher training, would spark greater fitness in kids at underserved schools. I think people appreciated this direct approach to a major societal problem. Second, our program was something all people could get behind, no matter what their politics or beliefs. Third, and most important, we have had terrific staff, generous donors, and deep community support to drive our success.

Given all we have been able to accomplish at UCLA Sound Body Sound Mind at a reasonable cost when prorated for the 750,000 students we have helped over the years, it is my great hope that others will follow our lead. We have a proven program that is well tested and scalable, ripe for replication anywhere.

Crucial takeaways

- There is quantifiable evidence that kids welcome and benefit from carefully crafted physical education programs. With the right curriculum, kids enjoy challenging themselves to improve their fitness levels.
- It is crucially important to develop relationships with knowledgeable people in the community who can help improve one's program.
- It is also important to build accountability into the gifting of a program like ours and to settle on the right set of requirements for recipients.

- Don't get stuck in a rut; be willing to make program adjustments as experience dictates.
- When individuals put their heads, hearts, and resources together to bring about change, great things happen!

Bill Simon rides on a spin bike, cheered on by his wife and cofounder, Cindy, during the official opening ceremony for a new fitness center at Alliance Ouchi O'Donovan 6-12 Complex.

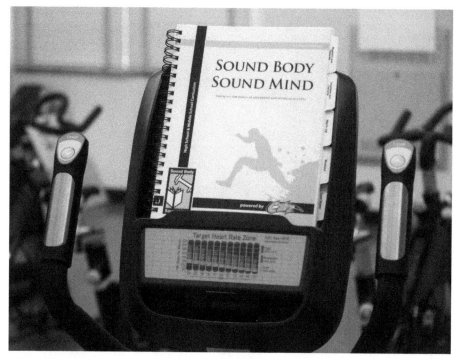

Developed in 2010, the Sound Body Sound Mind Curriculum was a major addition to the program, showing ways to create a safe and welcoming classroom environment while providing a number of structured lessons to engage large class sizes and keep students moving.

Middle school students at Porter Ranch Community School
show off big smiles on new spin bikes during the ribbon cutting
ceremony for their school's fitness center, opened in 2013.

Former CEO of UCLA Health, David Feinberg, and Cindy and Bill Simon show off the new UCLA Health Sound Body Sound Mind logo at the first ribbon cutting after both entities partnered together in March 2015.

Cindy and Bill Simon are pictured here with Rafer Johnson and his
wife, Betsy. Rafer, an Olympic gold medalist and UCLA athlete, served
as the keynote speaker at a 2015 fundraiser event celebrating the
partnership between UCLA Health and Sound Body Sound Mind.

A look inside the UCLA Health Sound Body Sound Mind fitness center at
Arleta High School, installed in 2016.
Every high school fitness center includes a mix of cardio and
strength training machines, as well as fitness accessories.

Physical education teachers and school administrators
cut the ribbon to officially open a new fitness center at
Los Angeles Academy Middle School in 2017.

Two middle school students at Marshall Academy of the Arts in
Long Beach high-five each other while working out on spin bikes.

Students from Thomas Starr King Middle School are recognized alongside UCLA Health Sound Body Sound Mind staff on court at the Staples Center during a Los Angeles Lakers basketball game in March 2018. Students were selected as the winners of the inaugural #TeamUCLALakers Challenge that highlighted students who had demonstrated a commitment to fitness and their local community.

A student from Miguel Contreras Learning Complex demonstrates an exercise from the Sound Body Sound Mind Curriculum.

High school students along with their physical education
teacher from Benjamin Franklin High School are pictured after
a demonstration of their new fitness center and curriculum
exercises during their ribbon cutting ceremony in 2018.

7

OPPORTUNITY KNOCKS: NEXT STEPS

Here are the facts. We know that physical fitness is essential to maintaining good health in our children. Conversely, we know that inactive children risk developing many serious diseases and disorders. Moreover, there is massive mounting evidence, as I have discussed, that exercise significantly bolsters mental well-being, social development, and academic achievement.

Fitness equips our children for life

I would argue that exercise is the only activity that engages and benefits the whole child: mind, body, and spirit. Fitness training is a vital part of equipping our children for life's challenges, every bit as important as the other things they learn in school, such as being able to read well or do the math to modify a recipe, calculate change, or pay taxes.

I think we can agree that fitness is the gateway to many good things we want for our kids. What parent does not want his or her child to lead a long and healthy life, learning persistence, resilience, and positive thinking along the way? Fitness activities are a practice field on which these character traits can be learned and honed.

Opportunity knocks in our schools

Sometimes opportunity stares you right in the face. The challenge is not in coming up with some brilliant new idea to fix a problem, but rather in implementing a known solution. I believe this is the case when it comes to addressing the inactivity epidemic that threatens our children's future.

We know of a place whose purpose is to educate and train children, where children spend a great deal of their time: school. So surely it is obvious that an important part of the solution to the inactivity pandemic is to be found there, in our nation's schools. I call physical education class the low-hanging fruit on the fitness tree, easily accessible for the maximum number of children.

Yes, parents must also take responsibility at home for their child's flourishing. But we have an incredible opportunity to help our children lead longer, healthier, and happier lives by insisting on more physical education in schools, and promoting a culture of movement there with opportunities for short bursts of exercise during the school day. This approach is practical and cost-effective, and it promises to transform lives for the better.

Traditionally, schools have been instrumental in supporting the good health of the children in attendance. They help to ensure students are immunized, provide health screenings, and strive to serve nutritional meals. Physical activity is every bit as essential to good health as well-balanced meals and the right shots, and it should be just as much a part of a school's mandate to promote healthy students.

Schools are not only the best place for children to become fit; they are also key to a fit future. According to the Physical Activity Council, children who have physical education in school are twice as likely to be active outside PE class and twice as likely to be active to a healthy level when they become adults.[1] While correlation does not equate to cause, it makes sense that children who learn good fitness habits in school will practice them out of school, and that a fit childhood sets a foundation for fitness as an adult.[2]

According to the National Education Association, "Physical education is an integral part of the total education of every child in kindergarten through high school. Quality physical education programs are needed to increase the physical competence, health-related fitness, self-responsibility, and enjoyment of physical activity for all students so they can be physically active for a lifetime."[3]

La Sierra High School's motivational magic

Imagine what could happen if our schools taught fitness to the level of La Sierra High School in Carmichael, California, circa 1962. A *Look* magazine article[4] that year describes the school's extraordinary physical education program, which challenged large groups of boys to progress through color-coded levels of fitness until they could do more pull-ups than were required for entrance to the United States Naval Academy. Developed by the school's PE teacher and football coach, Stan LeProtti, the program required no special equipment and little school time, but it was highly motivational; it was rigorous; and it focused on the fitness basics of strength, endurance, power, agility, and balance. Average kids excelled in it. Partly owing, no doubt, to the major emphasis President Kennedy placed on physical fitness, the program spread to four thousand high schools around the country and was adapted for girls.[5] Fitness expert Ron Jones, who himself participated in the same program at another high school, writes, "The La Sierra system only spent fifteen minutes per day on the vigorous fitness conditioning part of their curriculum ... How could these kids get so fit in fifteen minutes per day? *Focus.* They focused on quality ... So much for the naysayers regarding a lack of time to exercise!"[6]

La Sierra's extraordinary success and motivational magic are described in a 2017 award-winning film, *The Motivation Factor: PE 50 Years Ago,*[7] which explores the pivotal role PE plays in developing smart, productive, and mentally healthy citizens. I highly recommend it.

If we had more daily, vigorous, focused fitness programs in our schools today, just think about the potential impact on our kids and our country!

As the La Sierra experience shows, such programs do not have to be time consuming. The impact would be especially striking if rigorous physical education were accompanied by healthful eating and weight control. Instead of lamenting headlines that today's children may have shorter life expectancies than their parents, we'd be reading about their increased longevity. Type 2 diabetes would rarely be diagnosed at such tragically early ages, and cardiovascular health would improve. Children would do better in the classroom and learn strategies to help them run the obstacle course of adult life. And these are just a few of the benefits we'd reap. Our nation would be stronger because its population would be healthier in so many different ways, and the money spent treating diseases associated with inactivity could be deployed to greater advantage elsewhere.

Organizations on the move to improve physical education

While I am certainly alarmed about the state of physical education, I am a naturally glass-half-full kind of person who believes that optimism drives success. Happily, there are many positive developments taking place and many organizations working hard to improve the quality of physical education programs throughout the United States. If more of us catch their vision, our children will be much healthier. Some information follows about several such programs.

I have mentioned SHAPE America[8] a number of times in this book. Founded in 1885, SHAPE America is the nation's largest organization of health and PE professionals. Its mission is to advance professional practice and promote research related to health and physical education, physical activity, dance, and sport. It offers its members a wide variety of professional development opportunities to improve their skills as well as other programs to advance its vision of "a nation where all children are prepared to lead healthy, physically active lives." These include national and state-level conferences, detailed information on standards and grant funding, and guidance on advocacy efforts. In addition to the national organization, each state has its own affiliate chapter, providing more targeted local resources. My home state of California, for example, has CAHPERD, the California Association of Health, Physical Education, Recreation and Dance.

Another laudable program is the Presidential Youth Fitness Program (PYFP),[9] which we've also mentioned earlier in the book. Launched in 2012, the PYFP's primary goal is to promote quality fitness education and assessment practices. The PYFP provides schools across the country with a variety of resources, including professional development and instruction on implementing the Cooper Institute's FitnessGram assessment for students. It is managed and funded by the National Fitness Foundation, the only congressionally chartered nonprofit focused on health and fitness. Through their joint effort, more than 6,200 schools serving three million children in forty-seven states are learning how to empower students to be fit for life. Their work has been most helpful in promoting public-private partnerships to accelerate solutions that will give all children access to quality physical education.

The Alliance for a Healthier Generation[10] began as a project of the American Heart Association and the Clinton Foundation to act as a catalyst for children's health. It works with schools, companies, community organizations, health-care professionals, and families to reduce the prevalence of childhood obesity and to empower kids to develop lifelong, healthy habits. To this end, it seeks to transform the places kids spend their time into environments that encourage the healthiest lifestyles. Schools are, of course, a major focus of its programs, and it currently works with some thirty-one thousand schools nationwide on issues pertaining to wellness. The alliance's Healthy Schools Program provides tools, resources and training to help schools improve their physical education program as well as to create a more active environment within the classroom, during recess, and in out-of-school time before and after the official school day.

PHIT America[11] is a campaign dedicated to championing the benefits of fitness, increasing physical activity in schools, and educating about the perils of inactivity. With sponsorship and support from a number of top-tier sports-related companies such as Nike, Adidas, Under Armour, and New Balance, PHIT America has provided nearly three hundred schools with GO! Grants designed to increase physical activity in elementary schools.

The SPARK[12] program has also produced strong results. SPARK (Sports, Play, and Active Recreation for Kids) is an organization focused on providing evidence-based PE and health programs from pre-K through twelfth grades. A comprehensive SPARK physical education program includes a specialized curriculum, on-site training, specific equipment to execute the curriculum, and continued follow-up support. SPARK began its research on effective physical fitness programming in 1989 and today has trained teachers representing more than one hundred thousand schools worldwide. Combined with its outreach through workshops, conferences, and institutes, the SPARK program affects more than one million students every year.

Taking a lesson from the Big Apple

In May 2015, a report was published by the New York City Comptroller's office, titled *Dropping the Ball: Disparities in Physical Education in New York City Schools*.[13] In this report, a number of alarming discoveries were made, including the following:

- Over 32 percent of schools in New York lacked a full-time certified physical education teacher.
- Some 28 percent of schools in New York City lacked a dedicated "physical fitness space." Over 41 percent of high schools lacked this space, and more than 35 percent of middle schools had the same limitation.
- Nearly 10 percent of schools lacked both a full-time certified physical education teacher and dedicated physical fitness space.

This report, while disturbing, served to back up a number of others regarding the sorry state of physical education in New York City schools. While reports like these often are ignored, this time New York City reacted in a surprisingly positive way. After the results of this report went public, Mayor Bill de Blasio jumped into action, launching the PE Works program. During the 2015–2016 school year, $6 million was committed to piloting a new initiative in four hundred schools citywide to directly address shortfalls in physical education.[14] The city recognized that physical education was much more than a gym class and made fitness a new priority among public schools.

In this pilot year, a number of previous concerns were addressed. Fifty schools received funding for a certified and licensed physical education teacher.[15] Furthermore, the city implemented a program of professional development, engaging more than five hundred teachers in professional learning communities.[16] The initial funding also provided numerous grants for schools to start wellness councils and purchase the necessary equipment for a well-rounded physical education program.[17]

New York City has continued to invest in its students' future health, and it is a model for other cities. Following the success of year one, another $100 million was authorized to bring the PE Works model to all schools citywide.[18] Most recently, in June 2017, the city dedicated $385 million in capital funding to bring the necessary physical education space to lacking schools.[19]

A combination of programs at the national, state, and local levels are making a strong case for improved and increased physical education. Many helpful resources, ranging from curriculum design to professional development, are readily available to schools and teachers nationwide. The pool of research findings highlighting the multiple benefits of physical activity for students is continually growing. What is too often missing, however, is the will at the district levels to make physical fitness a priority in schools. This is why programs like Learning Readiness Physical Education in Naperville, PE Works in New York City, and UCLA Health Sound Body Sound Mind are so critically important; they demonstrate what we can achieve when we set our minds to it.

How to get involved

There is a lot readers can do to move the ball forward.

If you are the parent of a school-aged child, you could start by taking a physical education inventory at your school. SHAPE America publishes a helpful guide for parents about how to familiarize yourself with your child's PE program and includes a checklist of twelve helpful questions to ask.[20]

The Partnership for Prevention, a nonprofit organization dedicated to promoting health, has published an Action Guide[21] to help you work with schools in your community to implement more active PE classes. The systematic guide shows how to engage stakeholders, mount an effective outreach campaign, and identify a pilot school where the new PE program can be developed, showcased, and eventually publicized, serving as a springboard to district-wide implementation. The Action Guide also provides a list of experienced organizations to consult for additional information about building support for more active PE classes and to learn more about PE, physical activity, and school health issues.

Another valuable resource is the State Advocacy Toolkit on the website of SHAPE America.[22] If advocacy appeals to you more than local organizing, you will find a great deal there about legislation and policy, including helpful talking points and information about PE standards, key players, and education stakeholders in your state.

Together we can change the way schools regard physical education and move it up the curricular ladder to become an essential core subject. We know how to do it. All the resources are available. We simply need to summon up the most important ingredient: the will to make it happen. If we do this, if we make our children break a sweat every day, we will have gone a long way toward empowering them to lead the longer, stronger, healthier lives we all want for them.

Crucial takeaways

- Exercise is the only activity that engages and benefits the whole child: mind, body, and spirit. Fitness training is a vital part of equipping our children for life's challenges, every bit as important as being able to read a book or do the math to balance a checkbook.
- Schools are the best place to give our kids the fitness resources they need.
- We know how to improve PE; what is lacking is not the knowledge but the motivation to make fitness a priority in our schools.
- A number of national organizations that are wholly committed to improving physical education exist in the United States. The tools and resources are there!
- Working together, we can effect change, and we don't need to reinvent the wheel. Good model programs exist, like those in New York City, Los Angeles, and Naperville, Illinois, to learn from.

Afterword: The Eternal Triangle

This book has been a joy and a challenge to research and write—a joy because physical exercise has been important to me since childhood and the research has more than confirmed my instincts about its wide-ranging benefits. I want all people to know and experience this truth because it will make a fundamental and profound difference in their lives.

It has been a challenge because there is such a disconnect between this truth and the reality of life in the overwhelming majority of American schools. I feel a profound responsibility to set forth this dichotomy in an academically and empirically sound way, such that the policymakers and so-called education experts would have to face up to the errors of their ways and to the fact that they must bear responsibility for shortchanging our children, who are our future.

Physical education is a key component of any quality education, and our children have just as much of a right to physical literacy as they do to literacy in academic subjects.

I also feel a responsibility to stand up for physical education teachers who have been treated as second-class citizens by the educational establishment for decades. Their work is just as important as their academic brethren's is; indeed, they are also teachers in the best sense of that word.

Centuries of experience combined with the wonders of modern medical research confirm that there is a profound and fundamental connection between body, mind, and spirit. In ancient times, this unbreakable connection was sometimes referred to as the Eternal Triangle. Each leg of the triangle—body, mind, and spirit—is a separate concept, but each reinforces and strengthens the other two. In effect, one plus one plus equals four, or maybe even five.

For me, a beautiful day is one where I get some good exercise combining strength and cardio; where I am intellectually stimulated through work, a good book or a good movie; and where I have prayed, worshipped, or helped someone who couldn't pay me back. I usually sleep pretty well on those days.

Acknowledgments

Although my name appears as the author, this book is actually the product of the help and good counsel of many people.

At the top of the list is Caroline Hemphill, my longtime friend. Cary is gifted in many areas; she is a great writer, researcher, and wise counselor, among other strengths. She was intimately involved with every aspect of this book from start to finish and easily could have been named as coauthor.

Also heavily involved from beginning to end was Matthew Flesock, the executive director of UCLA Health Sound Body Sound Mind. Matt helped with conceptualization, research, and reviewing innumerable drafts. His colleagues, including Amanda Gittleman and Kayla Abeyta, provided similar important support.

I am very grateful to another longtime friend, James Piereson, president of the William E. Simon Foundation, for his excellent suggestion about how to structure the book.

My executive assistants, Denni Cohen and Tony Winston, shared their constructive criticism, and Tony brought his passion for physical fitness to bear on the manuscript with many hours of research.

Tami Georgeff offered advice on the book's design, and was instrumental in identifying a publisher, AuthorHouse, whose staff, including Dana Scott, Karen Stansberry, and Cynthia Wolfe, provided invaluable guidance.

Then, of course, as noted earlier, the book benefitted immensely from interviews with Christine Berni-Ramos, Dr. Frances Cleland, Dr. Kenneth Cooper, Dr. Jonathan Fielding, John Kruse, Dr. John Ratey, and Dr. Kimberly Uyeda. Dr. Cooper was also gracious enough to write the foreword to this book, for which I am most grateful.

Dr. Ming Guo and Dr. Wendy Suzuki (the chair and a member, respectively, of our Academic Advisory Council at UCLA Health Sound Body Sound Mind) also provided helpful comments, as did Olympic athlete John Naber.

I also appreciate the valuable assistance of our former executive directors: Emily Ernsdorf Fritz, Adrianna Johnson, Lindsay Payne, Scott MacKenzie, Keith Legro, Nathan Nambiar, and Patrick McCredie. Our program stands on their shoulders.

Finally, I want to thank Cindy, my wife of almost thirty-two years, for cofounding Sound Body Sound Mind with me in 1998. Her consistent enthusiasm, intelligence, and good sense underlie all our accomplishments, and we would not be celebrating twenty years in operation without her active participation in all aspects of our work.

I am deeply grateful to all the people mentioned above for their support of this project. All mistakes and shortcomings are my own.

Appendix A

SCHOOLS IN LOS ANGELES WITH UCLA HEALTH SOUND BODY SOUND MIND FITNESS CENTERS

1998
1. Palisades Charter High School

2000
2. St. Monica Catholic High School

2001
3. Venice Senior High School

2002
4. Garfield High School
5. Theodore Roosevelt High School
6. Susan Miller Dorsey High School
7. Santa Monica High School
8. John C. Fremont Senior High School

9. Verdugo Hills High School
10. Junipero Serra High School Center

2003
11. Thomas Jefferson Senior High School
12. James Monroe High School
13. Francis Polytechnic Senior High School

2004
14. Village Glen West School
15. University Senior High School
16. Bell Senior High School

2005
17. Joaquin Miller Career and Transition Center

18. North Hollywood Senior High School
19. Carson Senior High School
20. Wallis Annenberg School
21. Elizabeth Learning Center
22. Ernest P. Willenberg Special Education Center
23. Northridge Academy High School

2006

24. Alexander Hamilton Senior High School
25. Orthopaedic Hospital Medical Magnet High School
26. Reseda Senior High School
27. Diane S. Leichman Career Prep and Transition Center
28. Westchester Enriched Sciences Magnet School
29. George Washington Preparatory High School
30. San Fernando Senior High School
31. Sylmar Senior High School
32. Eagle Rock High School
33. John Marshall Senior High School
34. Woodrow Wilson Senior High School
35. Santee Education Complex
36. Grover Cleveland High School

2007

37. Van Nuys Senior High School

38. Charles Leroy Lowman Special Education Center
39. South Gate Senior High School
40. Benjamin Banneker Special Education Center
41. Chatsworth Charter Senior High School

2008

42. Frank D. Lanterman Special Education High School
43. Canoga Park Senior High School
44. William Howard Taft High School
45. San Pedro Senior High School
46. Manual Arts Senior High School
47. Alliance Gertz-Ressler High School
48. Joseph Pomeroy Widney High School
49. Gardena Senior High School
50. Alliance Dr. Olga Mohan High School
51. Ulysses S. Grant Senior High School

2009

52. Alliance Marc & Eva Stern Math and Science High School
53. Rudecinda Sepulveda Dodson Middle School
54. Alliance Richard Merkin Middle School

55. Northridge Middle School
56. William Jefferson Clinton
    Middle School
57. Marina Del Rey Middle School
58. Gaspar De Portola
    Middle School
59. Stephen M. White
    Middle School
60. Abraham Lincoln
    Senior High School

2010
61. Van Nuys Middle School
62. Pacific Boulevard School

2011
63. Alliance Cindy and
    Bill Simon Technology
    Academy High School
64. Vista Middle School
65. Alexander Fleming
    Middle School
66. Orville Wright Middle School
67. South Gate Middle School
68. Alfred B. Nobel Charter
    Middle School
69. D.W. Griffith Middle School
70. George K. Porter
    Middle School
71. Alliance Ouchi-O'Donovan
    6-12 Complex

2012
72. John Muir Middle School
73. Sun Valley Middle School

74. Robert E. Peary Middle School
75. Daniel Webster Middle School
76. Olive Vista Middle School
77. George Washington
    Carver Middle School
78. Dr. Mary McLeod
    Bethune Middle School
79. Felicitas & Gonzalo
    Mendez Learning Center

2013
80. Porter Ranch
    Community Schools
81. Dr. Julian Nava
    Learning Academy
82. Walnut Park Middle School
83. Mark Twain Middle School
84. Robert Lewis Stevenson
    Middle School
85. Sophia T. Salvin Special
    Education Center

2014
86. Alliance Susan and Eric Smidt
    Technology High School
87. Alliance Renee and Meyer
    Luskin Academy
88. James Madison Middle School
89. Sherman Oaks Center
    for Enriched Studies
90. Audubon Middle School

2015
91. Edwin Markham Middle School

92. Alliance Alice M. Baxter High School
93. Thomas Alva Edison Middle School
94. East Valley High School
95. Alfonso B. Perez Career and Transition Center
96. USC Hybrid High School

2016

97. Arleta High School
98. Nathaniel Narbonne High School
99. Belvedere Middle School
100. Christopher Columbus Middle School
101. Emerson Community Charter School
102. Joseph Le Conte Middle School
103. Berendo Middle School
104. Alliance Ted K. Tajima High School
105. Orchard Academy Middle School
106. Irving STEAM Middle School

2017

107. Los Angeles Academy Middle School
108. Nava College Prep Academy
109. Luther Burbank Middle School
110. Henry T. Gage Middle School
111. Thomas Starr King Middle School
112. John F. Kennedy High School

113. Walter Reed Middle School
114. Helen Bernstein High School
115. Francisco Sepulveda Middle School
116. Lincoln Middle School
117. John Adams Middle School

2018

118. El Sereno Middle School
119. Benjamin Franklin High School
120. Panorama High School
121. Culver City High School
122. Glenn Hammond Curtiss Middle School
123. Malibu High School
124. Palms Middle School
125. Alliance Marine Innovation & Technology 6-12 Complex
126. Marshall Academy of the Arts
127. Miguel Contreras Learning Complex

Appendix B

ADDITIONAL SCHOOLS SUPPORTED BY UCLA HEALTH SOUND BODY SOUND MIND

2009

Denver, Colorado

1. George Washington High School—Full Fitness Center
2. Abraham Lincoln High School—Full Fitness Center
3. Bruce Randolph School—Full Fitness Center
4. Denver Center for International Studies—Full Fitness Center
5. North High School—Full Fitness Center
6. West High School—Full Fitness Center
7. Martin Luther King, Jr. Early College—Full Fitness Center
8. John F. Kennedy High School—Full Fitness Center

2011

Dallas, Texas

9. Total of 218 schools in the Dallas Independent School District—Curriculum and SandBells

2012

Ave Maria, Florida

10. Rhodora J. Donahue Academy of Ave Maria—Full Fitness Center

2013

Los Angeles, California (UCLA Study)

11. Robert F. Kennedy Community Schools—Curriculum
     and Accessories

Camarillo, California

12. St. John's Seminary—Full Fitness Center

Oro Grande, California

13. Riverside Preparatory High School—Full Fitness Center

Bakersfield, California

14. Liberty High School—Full Fitness Center

2014

Los Angeles, California

15. Alliance Kory Hunter Middle School—Pilot Program

2016

San Jacinto, California

16. San Jacinto High School—Full Fitness Center

2017

East Sandwich, Massachusetts

17. Riverview School—Full Fitness Center

Appendix C

UCLA HEALTH SOUND BODY SOUND MIND
BOARD OF DIRECTORS, MAY 2018

Frank E. Baxter
Chairman Emeritus, Jefferies and Company

Henry J. Brandon
Director, Deal Structure and Risk, Nile Capital Group

Jesse Casso Jr.
Managing Partner, Casmar Capital Partners

Lance T. Izumi
Director of Center for School Reform, Pacific Research Institute

Jordan L. Kaplan
Chief Executive Officer, Douglas Emmett, Inc.

Keith R. Legro
Former Executive Director, Sound Body Sound Mind Foundation
Brand Manager, The Kraft Heinz Company

Jeffrey D. Lipp
Founder, The Kive Company

Nathan S. Nambiar
Former Executive Director, Sound Body Sound Mind Foundation
Vice President/Chief Operating Officer, Manifeste Marketing

J. Frederick Simmons
General Partner, Freeman Spogli & Co.

Cynthia L. Simon
Cofounder and President, Dollies Making a Difference

William E. Simon Jr.
Partner, Massey Quick Simon & Co.

Johnese Spisso
President, UCLA Health
Chief Executive Officer, UCLA Health System

Appendix D

UCLA HEALTH SOUND BODY SOUND MIND ACADEMIC ADVISORY COUNCIL, MAY 2018

Darla M. Castelli, PhD
Current organization: University of Texas at Austin
Department: Department of Kinesiology and Health Education
Position: Professor of Physical Education Pedagogy and Health Behavior

Eric Esrailian, MD, MPH
Current organization: Ronald Reagan UCLA Medical Center
Department: Medicine, Gastroenterology
Position: Cochief of the Division of Digestive Diseases

Jonathan E. Fielding, MD, MPH, MA, MBA
Current organization: UCLA Fielding School of Public Health
Department: Health Policy and Management
Position: Professor of Health Policy and Management, and Pediatrics

Ming Guo, MD, PhD
Current organization: UCLA David Geffen School of Medicine
Department: Neurology
Position: Professor in Neurology and Pharmacology

David R. McAllister, MD
Current organization: UCLA David Geffen School of Medicine
Department: Orthopaedic Surgery
Position: Professor of Orthopaedic Surgery. Also Head Team Physician for the LA Lakers and Associate Head Team Physician and Director of Orthopaedic Surgery for the UCLA Athletic Department

Henriette van Praag, PhD
Current organization: National Institutes of Health
Department: Laboratory of Neurology
Position: Investigator

Michael L. Prelip, MPH, DPA
Current organization: UCLA Fielding School of Public Health
Department: Community Health Sciences
Position: Professor and Chair, Department of Community Health Sciences

John J. Ratey, MD
Current organization: Harvard Medical School
Department: Psychiatry
Position: Associate Clinical Professor of Psychiatry

Wendy A. Suzuki, PhD
Current organization: New York University
Department: Center for Neural Science
Position: Professor of Neural Science and Psychology

Rachel Lyn Johnson Thornton, MD, PhD
Current organization: Johns Hopkins University School of Medicine
Department: Pediatrics
Position: Assistant Professor of Pediatrics

Endnotes

Introduction—Giving Kids the Chance They Deserve

1   Squash + Education Alliance, "By the Numbers," March 2, 2018. http://www.nationalurbansquash.org/about-us/by-the-numbers/.

2   *Shape of the Nation*, report, 2016, https://www.shapeamerica.org/uploads/pdfs/son/Shape-of-the-Nation-2016_web.pdf.

3   C. M. Hales, M. D. Carroll, C. D. Fryar, and C. L. Ogden, "Prevalence of Obesity among Adults and Youth: United States, 2015–2016," NCHS data brief, no 288. Hyattsville, MD, National Center for Health Statistics, 2017, https://www.cdc.gov/nchs/products/databriefs/db288.htm.

4   Li Yan Wang, David Chyen, Sarah Lee, and Richard Lowry, "The Association Between Body Mass Index in Adolescence and Obesity in Adulthood," *Journal of Adolescent Health* 42, no. 5 (2008): 512–18, doi:10.1016/j.jadohealth.2007.10.010.

5   S. Jay Olshansky, Douglas J. Passaro, Ronald C. Hershow, Jennifer Layden, Bruce A. Carnes, Jacob Brody, Leonard Hayflick, Robert N. Butler, David B. Allison, and David S. Ludwig, "A Potential Decline in Life Expectancy in the United States in the 21st Century," *New England Journal of Medicine* 352, no. 11 (2005): 1138–145, doi:10.1056/nejmsr043743.

6   Ibid.

7   "Physical Activity Guidelines for Americans," Guidelines Index—2008 Physical Activity Guidelines, 2008, https://health.gov/paguidelines/guidelines/.

8   "National Physical Activity Plan," Untitled Document, 2016, http://www.physicalactivityplan.org/projects/reportcard.html.

9   *Shape of the Nation*, report, 2016, https://www.shapeamerica.org/uploads/pdfs/son/Shape-of-the-Nation-2016_web.pdf.

10 John J. Ratey with Eric Hagerman, *Spark: The Revolutionary New Science of Exercise and the Brain*, New York, NY: Little, Brown, 2013.

Chapter 1—Sedentary Lifestyles and Unhealthy Eating: The Public Health Perspective

1   Charles M. Tipton, "The History of 'Exercise Is Medicine' in Ancient Civilizations," *Advances in Physiology Education* 38, no. 2 (2014): 109–17, doi:10.1152/advan.00136.2013.

2   Ibid.

3   Ibid.

4   Ibid.

5   Ibid.

6   Hippocrates, *On Regimen in Acute Diseases*, trans. W.H.S. Jones (1931), vol. 4, 229, quoted at https://todayinsci.com/H/Hippocrates/Hippocrates-Quotations.htm.

7   Charles M. Tipton, "The History of "Exercise Is Medicine" in Ancient Civilizations," *Advances in Physiology Education* 38, no. 2 (2014): 109–17, doi:10.1152/advan.00136.2013.

8   "The History of Fitness," www.ideafit.com, http://www.ideafit.com/fitness-library/the-history-of-fitness.

9   Heather L. Reid, "Sport and Moral Education in Plato's Republic," *Journal of the Philosophy of Sport* 34, no. 2 (2007): 160–75, doi:10.1080/00948705.2007.9714719.

10 Ibid.

11 "The History of Fitness," www.ideafit.com, http://www.ideafit.com/fitness-library/the-history-of-fitness.

12 Ibid.

13 Charles M. Tipton, "The History of 'Exercise Is Medicine' in Ancient Civilizations," *Advances in Physiology Education* 38, no. 2 (2014): 109–17, doi:10.1152/advan.00136.2013.

14 Paul M. Kennedy, *Grand Strategies in War and Peace*, New Haven: Yale University Press, 1992, p. 84–5.

15 "Thomas Jefferson's Monticello," Exercise | Thomas Jefferson's Monticello, https://www.monticello.org/site/research-and-collections/exercise#_note-2.

16 Jonathan Fielding, Personal interview, Los Angeles, January 30, 2018.

17 Jonathan Fielding, "There's Always So Much More to Do," Faculty profile, https://ph.ucla.edu/sites/default/files/downloads/magazine/sphmag.6.12.fieldingprofile.web_.pdf.

18 Southern California Public Radio, "Head of LA County Health Department, Jonathan Fielding, to resign," March 27, 2014, http://www.scpr.org/news/2014/03/27/43090/head-of-la-county-health-department-dr-jonathan-fi/.

19 Jonathan Fielding, "The New Surgeon General Can Make a Real Impact in Reducing the Number of Overweight Kids," *U.S. News and World Report*, July

26, 2017, https://www.usnews.com/opinion/policy-dose/articles/2017-07-26/new-us-surgeon-general-to-be-jerome-adams-can-combat-childhood-obesity.

20 Centers for Disease Control and Prevention, "Diabetes," PDF, 2016, https://www.cdc.gov/chronicdisease/resources/publications/aag/diabetes.htm.

21 Jonathan Fielding, "Our Lifestyles Are Killing Us," *U.S. News and World Report*, November 16, 2017, https://www.usnews.com/opinion/policy-dose/articles/2017-11-16/americans-must-change-our-unhealthy-lifestyles-to-combat-type-2-diabetes.

22 Ibid.

23 Jonathan Fielding, "Obesity and Related Mortality in Los Angeles," report, County of Los Angeles Public Health, Los Angeles, CA: County of Los Angeles Public Health, 2011, http://publichealth.lacounty.gov/ha/reports/habriefs/2007/Obese_Cities/Obesity_2011Fs.pdf.

24 Tanja V. E. Kral, Jesse Chittams, and Reneé H. Moore, "Relationship between Food Insecurity, Child Weight Status, and Parent-Reported Child Eating and Snacking Behaviors," *Journal for Specialists in Pediatric Nursing* 22, no. 2 (2017), doi:10.1111/jspn.12177.

25 Jonathan Fielding, Personal interview, Los Angeles, CA: January 30, 2018.

26 Ibid.

27 Ibid.

28 Ibid.

29 Al Baker, "Despite Obesity Concerns, Gym Classes Are Cut," the *New York Times*, July 10, 2012, http://www.nytimes.com/2012/07/11/education/even-as-schools-battle-obesity-physical-education-is-sidelined.html?mcubz=1.

30 Kimbro, Rachel et all, "Young Children in Urban Areas: Links among Neighborhood Characteristics, Weight Status, Outdoor Play, and Television Watching," *Social Science & Medicine* 72, no. 5 (2011): 668–76, doi:10.1016/j.socscimed.2010.12.015.

31 N. McDonald, "Active Transportation to School Trends Among U.S. Schoolchildren, 1969–2001," *American Journal of Preventive Medicine* 32, no. 6 (2007): 509–16, doi:10.1016/j.amepre.2007.02.022.

32 Blake Williams, "Youth Sports Participation Continues to Decline and Congress May Have a Solution," *Forbes*, June 15, 2016, https://www.forbes.com/sites/blakewilliams3012/2016/06/15/youth-sports-participation-continues-to-decline-and-congress-may-have-a-solution/#1cd81e49177d.

33 The Cooper Institute, "Cooper Institute Advocacy Initiatives," http://www.cooperinstitute.org/advocacy-initiatives.

34 Centers for Disease Control and Prevention, "Childhood Obesity Facts," April 10, 2017, https://www.cdc.gov/obesity/data/childhood.html.

35 John Maynard Keynes, *Essays in Persuasion*, New York, NY: Classic House Books, 2009, p. 199.

36   Christopher Ingraham, "Nearly One[-]Third of the American Labor Force Works on the Weekend," the *Washington Post*, September 8, 2014. https://www.washingtonpost.com/news/wonk/wp/2014/09/08/nearly-one-third-of-the-american-labor-force-works-on-the-weekend/?tid=a_inl&utm_term=.c158e2fd4c1a.

37   Common Sense Media: Ratings, Reviews, and Advice, "Media Use by Tweens and Teens: Infographic | Common Sense Media," https://www.commonsensemedia.org/the-common-sense-census-media-use-by-tweens-and-teens-infographic.

38   Jonathan Fielding, "The New Surgeon General Can Make a Real Impact in Reducing the Number of Overweight Kids," *U.S. News and World Report*, July 26, 2017, https://www.usnews.com/opinion/policy-dose/articles/2017-07-26/new-us-surgeon-general-to-be-jerome-adams-can-combat-childhood-obesity.

39   Jonathan Fielding, Personal interview, Los Angeles, January 30, 2018.

40   Bruce Y. Lee, Atif Adam, Eli Zenkov, Daniel Hertenstein, Marie C. Ferguson, Peggy I. Wang, Michelle S. Wong, Patrick Wedlock, Sindiso Nyathi, Joel Gittelsohn, Saeideh Falah-Fini, Sarah M. Bartsch, Lawrence J. Cheskin, and Shawn T. Brown, "Modeling the Economic and Health Impact of Increasing Children's Physical Activity in the United States," *Health Affairs* 36, no. 5 (2017): 902-08. doi:10.1377/hlthaff.2016.1315.

41   Ibid.

42   Jonathan Fielding, Personal interview, Los Angeles, January 30, 2018.

43   Kimberly E. Uyeda, Personal interview, Los Angeles, January 18, 2018.

44   "Michelle King," Ed-Data, http://www.ed-data.org/district/Los-Angeles/Los-Angeles-Unified.

45   RAND Corporation, "Middle School Intervention Program Leads to Long-Term BMI Reduction for Obese Students," https://www.rand.org/news/press/2016/05/23.html#.

46   Joseph A. Ladapo, Laura M. Bogart, David J. Klein, Burton O. Cowgill, Kimberly E. Uyeda, David G. Binkle, Elizabeth R. Stevens, and Mark A. Schuster, "Cost and Cost-Effectiveness of Students for Nutrition and Exercise (SNaX)," RAND Corporation, April 28, 2016, https://www.rand.org/pubs/external_publications/EP66450.html.

47   Kimberly E. Uyeda, Personal interview, Los Angeles, January 18, 2018.

48   Ibid.

Chapter 2 – Deadly Duo: Inactivity and Obesity

1   Kenneth H. Cooper, Telephone interview, January 11, 2018.

2   Ibid.

3   Kenneth H. Cooper, *Aerobics*, New York, NY: Bantam Books, 1969.

4   Cheryl Hall, "'Health Missionary': Dallas' Father of Aerobics Reaching out to China's 300 Million Obese," *Dallas News*, June 8, 2017, https://www.dallasnews.com/business/business/2017/06/08/western-ways-gave-china-obesity-epidemic-thefather-aerobics-comes-rescue.

5   The Cooper Institute, "Cooper Institute Advocacy Initiatives," 2014, http://www.cooperinstitute.org/advocacy/.

6   Kenneth H. Cooper, Telephone interview, January 11, 2018.

7   American Heart Association, "Children's Cardiovascular Fitness Declining—Go Red for Women," Go Red For Women®, January 13, 2014, https://www.goredforwomen.org/about-heart-disease/heart_disease_research-subcategory/childrens-cardiovascular-fitness-declining/.

8   National Center for Health Statistics, *Health, United States, 2016: With Chartbook on Long-term Trends in Health,* 2017, https://www.cdc.gov/nchs/data/hus/hus16.pdf.

9   Kenneth H. Cooper, Telephone interview, January 11, 2018.

10   Steatohepatitis, Division of Gastroenterology, Hepatology and Nutrition, "Steatohepatitis Center," 2018, https://www.cincinnatichildrens.org/service/s/steatohepatitis.

11   Jonathan Sorof and Stephen Daniels, "Obesity Hypertension in Children," *Hypertension* 40 (October 1, 2002): 441–47, doi:https://doi.org/10.1161/01.HYP.0000032940.33466.12.

12   Kenneth H. Cooper, Telephone interview, January 11, 2018.

13   World Health Organization, "Obesity and Overweight," February 2018, http://www.who.int/mediacentre/factsheets/fs311/en/.

14   Kenneth H. Cooper, Telephone interview, January 11, 2018.

15   Ibid.

16   Paul W. Franks, Robert L. Hanson, William C. Knowler, Maurice L. Sievers, Peter H. Bennett, and Helen C. Looker, "Childhood Obesity, Other Cardiovascular Risk Factors, and Premature Death," *New England Journal of Medicine* 362, no. 6 (February 11, 2010): 485–93, doi:10.1056/nejmoa0904130.

17   C. Brooke Steele, Cheryll C. Thomas, S. Jane Henley, Greta M. Massetti, Deborah A. Galuska, Tanya Agurs-Collins, Mary Puckett, and Lisa C. Richardson, "Vital Signs: Trends in Incidence of Cancers Associated with Overweight and Obesity—United States, 2005–2014," *MMWR, Morbidity and Mortality Weekly Report* 66, no. 39 (October 3, 2017): 1052–058, doi:10.15585/mmwr.mm6639e1.

18   National Cancer Institute, "Obesity and Cancer," January 2017, https://www.cancer.gov/about-cancer/causes-prevention/risk/obesity/obesity-fact-sheet.

19   World Health Organization, *Global Recommendations on Physical Activity for Health*, 2010. http://www.who.int/dietphysicalactivity/global-PA-recs-2010.pdf

20   Kristi B. Adamo, Nick Barrowman, Patti Jean Naylor, Sanni Yaya, Alysha Harvey, Kimberly P. Grattan, and Gary S. Goldfield. "Activity Begins in Childhood (ABC)—Inspiring Healthy Active Behaviour in Preschoolers: Study

Protocol for a Cluster Randomized Controlled Trial," *Trials*, July 29, 2014, https://trialsjournal.biomedcentral.com/articles/10.1186/1745-6215-15-305.

21 The Cooper Institute," "Cooper Institute Advocacy Initiatives," 2014, http://www.cooperinstitute.org/advocacy/.

22 Generation Inactive, report, "UK Active Kids," May 15, 2015, *http://www.ukactive.com/downloads/managed/ON02629_UK_Active_Kids_report_online_spreads_FP.PDF.*

23 National Cancer Institute, "NIH Study Finds Leisure-Time Physical Activity Extends Life Expectancy as Much as 4.5 Years," News release, November 6, 2012.

24 Kenneth H. Cooper, Telephone interview, January 11, 2018.

25 WHO, "Physical Activity and Adults," http://www.who.int/dietphysicalactivity/factsheet_adults/en/.

26 Centers for Disease Control and Prevention, "How Much Physical Activity Do Children Need?", June 4, 2015, https://www.cdc.gov/physicalactivity/basics/children/index.htm.

27 Kenneth H. Cooper, Telephone interview, January 11, 2018.

28 Aspen Institute, "Physical Literacy in the United States: A Model, Strategic Plan, and Call to Action," 2017.

29 Centers for Disease Control and Prevention, "Healthy Schools," January 29, 2018, https://www.cdc.gov/healthyschools/obesity/facts.htm.

30 Kenneth H. Cooper, Telephone interview, January 11, 2018.

31 National Physical Activity Plan, "The 2016 United States Report Card on Physical Activity for Children and Youth," 2016, http://www.physicalactivityplan.org/reportcard/2016FINAL_USReportCard.pdf

32 Physical Activity | Healthy People 2020, "Physical Activity," https://www.healthypeople.gov/2020/topics-objectives/topic/physical-activity/national-snapshot.

33 I-Min Lee, Eric J. Shiroma, Felipe Lobelo, Pekka Puska, Steven N. Blair, and Peter T. Katzmarzyk, "Impact of Physical Inactivity on the World's Major Non-Communicable Diseases," *Lancet* 380, no. 9838 (July 21, 2012): 219–29, doi:10.1016/S0140-6736(12)61031-9.

34 Ibid.

35 Kenneth H. Cooper, Telephone interview, January 11, 2018.

36 The Cooper Institute, "About FitnessGram®," http://www.cooperinstitute.org/fitnessgram.

37 Eunice Kennedy Shriver National Institute of Child Health and Human Development, "How does physical activity help build healthy bones?", December 1, 2016. https://www.nichd.nih.gov/health/topics/bonehealth/conditioninfo/activity.

38 The Cooper Institute, "Healthy Fitness Zone® Standards," http://www.cooperinstitute.org/fitnessgram/standards.

39   The Cooper Institute, "Why FitnessGram®?", http://www.cooperinstitute. org/fitnessgram/why.

40   Kenneth H. Cooper, Telephone interview, January 11, 2018.

41   The Cooper Institute, "Texas Education Agency Releases FITNESSGRAM® Results—Cooper Institute," http://www.cooperinstitute.org/pub/news.cfm? id=47.

42   Pam Czerlinsky, "FitnessGram," E-mail message to author, February 9, 2018.

43   Ross C. Brownson, Tegan K. Boehmer, and Douglas A. Luke, "Declining Rates of Physical Activity in the United States: What Are the Contributors?", *Annual Review of Public Health* 26, no. 1 (2005): 421–43. doi:10.1146/annurev.publhealth.26. 021304.144437.

44   Ibid.

45   Kenneth H. Cooper, Telephone interview, January 11, 2018.Cooper, Kenneth H. Telephone interview, January 11, 2018.

46   Ibid.

47   A. Y. Sim, K. E. Wallman, T. J. Fairchild, and K. J. Guelfi, "High-Intensity Intermittent Exercise Attenuates Ad-Libitum Energy Intake," *International Journal of Obesity* 38, no. 3 (2013): 417–22, doi:10.1038/ijo.2013.102.

48   Kenneth H. Cooper, Telephone interview, January 11, 2018.

49   United States Office of Disease Prevention and Health Promotion, Physical Activity Guidelines for Adults, https://health.gov/paguidelines/guidelines/ children.aspx.

50   Ibid.

51   Kenneth H. Cooper, Telephone interview, January 11, 2018.

Chapter 3—Exercise: "Miracle-Gro for the Brain"

1   John J. Ratey, Personal interview, Los Angeles, January 18, 2018.

2   Ibid.

3   Ibid.

4   Ibid.

5   Edward Hallowell in a review of *Spark* posted on Amazon.com, https://www. amazon.com/Spark-Revolutionary-Science-Exercise-Brain/dp/0316113514/ref =sr_1_1?ie=UTF8&qid=1521214933&sr=8-1&keywords=ratey

6   John J. Ratey, Personal interview, Los Angeles, January 18, 2018.

7   Ibid.

8   John J. Ratey with Eric Hagerman, *Spark: The Revolutionary New Science of Exercise and the Brain*, New York, NY: Little, Brown, 2013, p. 12.

9   Ibid.

10   John J. Ratey, Personal interview, Los Angeles, January 18, 2018.

11   Lifetime Daily. "Authority on the Brain Explains the Life-Changing Effects of Exercise," January 31, 2018, https://www.lifetimedaily.com/brain-experts-explains-the-life-changing-effects-of-exercise/.

12   John J. Ratey with Eric Hagerman, *Spark: The Revolutionary New Science of Exercise and the Brain*, New York, NY: Little, Brown, 2013, p. 53.

13   John J. Ratey, Personal interview, Los Angeles, January 18, 2018.

14   Wendy Suzuki with Billie Fitzpatrick, *Healthy Brain, Happy Life: A Personal Program to Activate Your Brain and Do Everything Better*, New York, NY: Dey St., an imprint of William Morrow Publishers, 2016.

15   "We increase our use of brain cells in …" Rick Hanson, PhD, https://www.facebook.com/rickhansonphd/videos/937954469700570/.

16   Charles Hillman, Matthew Pontifex, Darla Castelli, Naiman Khan, Lauren Raine, Mark Scudder, Eric Drollette, Robert Moore, Chien-Ting Wu, and Keita Kamijo, "Effects of the FITKids Randomized Controlled Trial on Executive Control and Brain Function," *Pediatrics* 134, no. 4 (2014), doi:10.1542/peds.2013-3219d.

17   Tara Haelle, "After-School Exercise Yields Brain Gains: Study," WebMD, September 29, 2014, https://www.webmd.com/fitness-exercise/news/20140929/after-school-exercise-yields-brain-gains-study#1.

18   David Phillips, James C. Hannon, and Darla M. Castelli, "Effects of Vigorous Intensity Physical Activity on Mathematics Test Performance," *Journal of Teaching in Physical Education* 34, no. 3 (2015): 346–62, doi:10.1123/jtpe.2014-0030.

19   Science Daily, "Physical Activity May Strengthen Children's Ability to Pay Attention," PDF, April 1, 1999.

20   Matthew B. Pontifex, Brian J. Saliba, Lauren B. Raine, Daniel L. Picchietti, and Charles H. Hillman, "Exercise Improves Behavioral, Neurocognitive, and Scholastic Performance in Children with Attention-Deficit/Hyperactivity Disorder," *The Journal of Pediatrics* 162, no. 3 (2013): 543–51, doi:10.1016/j.jpeds.2012.08.036.

21   Mayo Clinic, "Exercise and Stress: Get Moving to Manage Stress," March 8, 2018, http://www.mayoclinic.org/healthy-lifestyle/stress-management/in-depth/exercise-and-stress/art-20044469.

22   Nadine Burke Harris, *The Deepest Well: Healing the Long-Term Effects of Childhood Adversity*, New York, NY: Houghton Mifflin Harcourt Publishing Company, 2018.

23   David Bornstein, "Treating the Lifelong Harm of Childhood Trauma," the *New York Times*, January 30, 2018, https://www.nytimes.com/2018/01/30/opinion/treating-the-lifelong-harm-of-childhood-trauma.html.

24   Deborah Gage, "Exercise Has a Cascade of Positive Effects, Study Finds," *Wall Street Journal*, June 26, 2017.

25   John J. Ratey, Personal interview, Los Angeles, January 18, 2018.

26 Ceylan Yeginsu, "U.K. Appoints a Minister for Loneliness," the *New York Times*, January 17, 2018, https://www.nytimes.com/2018/01/17/world/europe/uk-britain-loneliness.html.

27 UPI, "NIH: Autism rates in U.S. appear to be stabilizing," January 2, 2018. https://www.upi.com/Health_News/2018/01/02/NIH-Autism-rates-in-US-appear-to-be-stabilizing/2101514927151/.

28 Physical Exercise and Autism | Autism Research Institute, http://www.autism.com/treating_exercise.

29 Republished with permission of National Academies Press, from *Educating the Student Body: Taking Physical Activity and Physical Education to School*, Heather Cook, 2013; permission conveyed through Copyright Clearance Center, Inc. doi:10.17226/18314.

30 John J. Ratey, Personal interview, Los Angeles, January 18, 2018.

Chapter 4—Report Card: The State of Physical Education in American Schools Today

1 "President John Fitzgerald Kennedy Film on Physical Fitness, 30 March 1962," YouTube video, 2:31, Posted by YouTube, March 30, 2013. https://www.youtube.com/watch?v=8Dt4sczXYc8.

2 John F. Kennedy, "The Soft American," *Sports Illustrated*, December 26, 1960, 15–17, https://www.si.com/vault/issue/43278/17/2.

3 Presidential Youth Fitness Program, "Champion Fitness. Champion Kids. Parent Resource Guide to the Presidential Youth Fitness Program," https://www.pyfp.org/doc/parent-guide.pdf.

4 National Center for Education Statistics, "Fast Facts," https://nces.ed.gov/fastfacts/display.asp?id=66.

5 David L. Gallahue and Frances Cleland Donnelly, *Developmental Physical Education for All Children: Theory into Practice*, 5th Edition, Champaign, IL: Human Kinetics, 2015.

6 Frances Cleland, Telephone interview, January 31, 2018.

7 E. Paul Roetert, Dean Kriellaars, Todd S. Ellenbecker, and Cheryl Richardson, "Preparing Students for a Physically Literate Life," *Journal of Physical Education, Recreation & Dance*, vol. 88, no. 1 (2017): 57–62, doi:10.1080/07303084.2017.1252554.

8 Ibid.

9 Frances Cleland, Telephone interview, January 31, 2018.

10 Ibid.

11 Mark Hyman, "The Troubling Price of Playing Youth Sports," The Conversation, June 3, 2015, https://theconversation.com/the-troubling-price-of-playing-youth-sports-38191.

12   "AAP recommends delaying specialization until age 15," National Alliance for Youth Sports, September 2, 2016, https://www.nays.org/sklive/sure-shots/aap-recommends-delaying-specialization-until-age-15/.

13   Frances Cleland, Telephone interview, January 31, 2018.

14   T. Tompson et al, "Obesity in the United States: Public Perceptions," The Associated Press-NORC Center for Public Affairs Research, 2013, http://www.apnorc.org/PDFs/Obesity/AP-NORC-Obesity-Research-Highlights.pdf.

15   Republished with permission of National Academies Press, from *Educating the Student Body: Taking Physical Activity and Physical Education to School*, Heather Cook, 2013; permission conveyed through Copyright Clearance Center, Inc., doi:10.17226/18314.

16   Carly Wright, "What's Next with ESSA," SHAPE America, December 23, 2015. http://community.shapeamerica.org/blogs/carly-braxton/2015/12/23/whats-next-with-essa.

17   U.S. Department of Education, "U.S. Department of Education Awards More Than $24 million to Local Education Agencies and Community-based Organizations for Physical Education and Nutrition Education," October 7, 2016, https://www.ed.gov/news/press-releases/us-department-education-awards-more-24-million-local-education-agencies-and-community-based-organizations-physical-education-and-nutrition-education.

18   *Shape of the Nation*, report, 2016, http://www.shapeamerica.org/advocacy/son/2016/upload/Shape-of-the-Nation-2016_web.pdf.

19   U.S. Department of Health and Human Services, "Strategies to Improve the Quality of Physical Education," Report, 2010, https://www.cdc.gov/healthyschools/pecat/quality_pe.pdf.

20   Ibid.

21   Gregor Starc and Janko Strel, "Influence of the quality implementation of a physical education curriculum on the physical development and the physical fitness of children," *BMC Public Health*, January 20, 2012, https://doi.org/10.1186/1471-2458-12-61.

22   *Shape of the Nation*, report, 2016, https://www.shapeamerica.org/uploads/pdfs/son/Shape-of-the-Nation-2016_web.pdf.

23   Ibid.

24   U.S. Department of Health and Human Services, *Youth Risk Behavior Surveillance—United States, 2015*, report, 6th ed., vol. 65, 2016.

25   Laura Segal, Jack Rayburn, and Alejandra Martin, *The State of Obesity 2016*, Trust for America's Health, http://healthyamericans.org/reports/stateofobesity2016/.

Chapter 5—Let's Get Physical: Two Physical Educators Share Their Perspectives

1   Christine Berni-Ramos, Personal interview, Los Angeles, January 19, 2018.

2   Ibid.

3   John Kruse, Email message to author, March 5, 2018.

4   Lynn Couturier MacDonald, Robert John Doan, and Stevie Chepko, *Lesson Planning for High School Physical Education: Meeting the National Standards & Grade-Level Outcomes*, Champaign, IL: Human Kinetics, 2018.

5   John Kruse, Personal interview, Los Angeles, January 18, 2018.

6   Christine Berni-Ramos, Personal interview, Los Angeles, January 19, 2018.

7   John Kruse, Personal interview, Los Angeles, January 18, 2018.

8   Ibid.

9   Ibid.

10   Christine Berni-Ramos, Personal interview, Los Angeles, January 19, 2018.

11   Ibid.

12   John Kruse, Personal interview, Los Angeles, January 18, 2018.

13   "Physical Fitness Test." California Department of Education. https://dq.cde.ca.gov/dataquest/PhysFitness/PFTDN/Summary2011.aspx?r=0&t=2&y=2016-17&c=19647330000000&n=0000.

14   John Kruse, Personal interview, Los Angeles, January 18, 2018.

15   Christine Berni-Ramos, Personal interview, Los Angeles, January 19, 2018.

16   Ibid.

17   Kimberly E. Uyeda, Personal interview, Los Angeles, January 18, 2018.

18   See Brennan Davis and Christopher Carpenter, "Proximity of Fast-Food Restaurants to Schools and Adolescent Obesity," *American Journal of Public Health* 99, no. 3 (March 1, 2009): pp. 505–510. See also Philip H. Howard, Margaret Fitzpatrick, and Brian Fulfrost, "Proximity of Food Retailers to Schools and Rates of Overweight Ninth[-]Grade Students: An Ecological Study in California," *BMC Public Health,* 2011, vol. 11, number 1, page 1; Susan H. Babey, Joelle Wolstein, and Allison L. Diamant, "Food Environments Near Home and School Related to Consumption of Soda and Fast Food," *Health Policy Brief,* UCLA Center for Health Policy Research, July 2011.

19   John Kruse, Personal interview, Los Angeles, January 18, 2018.

20   Christine Berni-Ramos, Personal interview, Los Angeles, January 19, 2018.

21   Ibid.

Chapter 6—Break a Sweat, Change Your Life: The Story of UCLA Health Sound Body Sound Mind

1   Anna Gorman, "Childhood Obesity Rates Level off in California, L.A. County," *Los Angeles Times*, November 10, 2011, http://articles.latimes.com/2011/nov/10/local/la-me-childhood-obesity-20111110.

2   "Key Indicators of Health," Los Angeles County Department of Public Health, Office of Health Assessment and Epidemiology, March 2013, http://publichealth.lacounty.gov/docs/HealthNews/KeyIndicators-3-13.pdf.

3   Louise Johnson-Down, Jennifer O'Loughlin, Kristine G. Koski, and Katherine Gray-Donald, "High Prevalence of Obesity in Low Income and Multiethnic Schoolchildren: A Diet and Physical Activity Assessment," *The Journal of Nutrition* 127, no. 12 (December 1997): 2310–315, doi:https://doi.org/10.1093/jn/127.12.2310.

4   Emily Fritz, Email to the author, June 26, 2017.

5   Adrianna Johnson, Written interview with author, June 2017.

6   Keith Legro, Telephone interview, June 7, 2017.

7   Anastasia Loukaitou-Sideris, "Targeting the Body and the Mind: Evaluation of a P.E. Curriculum Intervention for Adolescents," *Journal of Education and Training Studies* 3, no. 4 (2015), doi:10.11114/jets.v3i4.873.

8   UCLA Health, "About Us: Best Healthcare, Latest Medical Technology," https://www.uclahealth.org/about-us.

9   "Top 10 Female Sports Pioneers," November 23, 2008, http://keepingscore.blogs.time.com/2008/11/23/top-10-female-sports-pioneers/slide/ann-meyers-drysdale/.

10 David Feinberg, "Getting to the Core of Childhood Obesity," March 12, 2015, https://health.usnews.com/health-news/blogs/eat-run/2015/03/12/getting-to-the-core-of-childhood-obesityFielding,

11 Benjamin Davies, Nathan Nambiar, Caroline Hemphill, Elizabeth Devietti, Alexandra Massengale, and Patrick McCredie, "Intrinsic Motivation in Physical Education," *Journal of Physical Education, Recreation & Dance* 86, no. 8 (2015): 8–13, doi:10.1080/07303084.2015.1075922.

12 Videos about the UCLA Health Sound Body Sound Mind program may be accessed at www.soundbodysoundmind.org.

13 Christine Berni-Ramos, Personal interview, Los Angeles, January 19, 2018.

14 John Kruse, Personal interview, Los Angeles, January 18, 2018.

15 Keith Bernas, Email to the author, January 16, 2018.

Chapter 7—Opportunity Knocks: Next Steps

1   *Participation Report.* Physical Activity Council, 2018, http://physicalactivitycouncil. com/pdfs/current.pdf.

2   Stephen M. Miller and Jason T. Siegel, "Youth Sports and Physical Activity: The Relationship between Perceptions of Childhood Sport Experience and Adult Exercise Behavior," *Psychology of Sport and Exercise* 33 (2017): 85–92, doi:10.1016/j.psychsport.2017.08.009.

3   Charlotte Kelso, "The Importance of Physical Education," http://www.veanea. org/home/1000.htm.

4   "La Sierra High School Shows How American Can Get Physically Tough," *Look* magazine, January 30, 1962, http://theleanberets.com/wp-content/ uploads/2012/12/la-sierra-article.pdf

5   Mental Floss, "This 1960s High School Gym Class Would Ruin You," April 13, 2015, http://mentalfloss.com/article/62991/1960s-high-school-gym-class-would-ruin-you.

6   "La Sierra High PE-Past Lessons for Future Fitness," The Lean Berets, http:// theleanberets.com/la-sierra-high-pe-past-lessons-for-future-fitness.

7   For more information, see: www.motivationmovie.com.

8   For more information, see: www.shapeamerica.org.

9   For more information, see: www.pyfp.org.

10   For more information, see: www.healthiergeneration.org.

11   For more information, see: www.phitamerica.org.

12   For more information, see: www.sparkpe.org.

13   Office of New York City Comptroller Scott M. Stringer, *Dropping the Ball: Disparities in Physical Education in New York City*, https://comptroller.nyc.gov/ reports/dropping-the-ball-disparities-in-physical-education-in-new-york-city/.

14   NYC Department of Education, *Revitalizing Physical Education in New York City Schools*, report, http://schools.nyc.gov/NR/rdonlyres/5BD34CD6-D413-47A2-8742-9FB42602EFBE/0/DOEPEWorksReportforYear1201516_APPROVED.pdf.

15   Ibid.

16   Ibid.

17   Ibid.

18   Ibid.

19   Official website of the City of New York, "Mayor de Blasio Announces Universal Physical Education Initiative," June 5, 2017, http://www1.nyc.gov/ office-of-the-mayor/news/390-17/mayor-de-blasio-speaker-mark-viverito-chancellor-fari-a-universal-physical-education#/0.

20   SHAPE America, "Getting to Know Your Child's PE Program," PDF, 2017, https://www.shapeamerica.org/uploads/pdfs/2017/downloads/eguides/ Parent_Checklist.pdf.

21   Centers for Disease Control and Prevention, *Working with Schools to Increase Physical Activity among Children and Adolescents in Physical Education Classes*, https://sparkpe.org/wp-content/uploads/2010/01/CDC_PE_Action_Guide.pdf.

22   SHAPE America, "Advocacy," State Standards & Advocacy Toolkits, https://www.shapeamerica.org/advocacy/advocacyresources_state.aspx.

About the Author

William E. Simon Jr. is chair of UCLA Health Sound Body Sound Mind, a nonprofit organization he cofounded in 1998 to combat childhood obesity by placing fitness equipment in schools. He has been active on the boards of a number of charitable organizations concerned with children's health and well-being. He is also a partner in Massey Quick Simon, an independent wealth management firm, and an adjunct professor in UCLA's law school and economics department. A former Republican nominee for governor in California, he lives with his wife, Cindy, in Los Angeles. They have four grown children.

CPSIA information can be obtained
at www.ICGtesting.com
Printed in the USA
BVHW09*0025110718
521311BV00003B/3/P

9 781546 243663